OVERCOMING ANGER

How to
Identify It,
Stop It,
and
Live a
Healthier
Life

By Carol D. Jones, Ph.D., M.F.T.

D0108257

ADAMS MEDIA
Avon, Massachusetts

Published by
Adams Media, an F+W Publications Company
57 Littlefield Street, Avon, MA 02322. U.S.A.
www.adamsmedia.com

ISBN: 1-58062-929-6

Printed in the United States of America.

J I H G F E D C B

Library of Congress Cataloging-in-Publication Data
Jones, Carol D.
Overcoming anger / Carol D. Jones.
p.   cm.
Includes bibliographical references and index.
ISBN 1-58062-929-6
1. Anger. I. Title.

BF575.A5J66 2004
152.4'7--dc21
2003008261

This publication is designed to provide accurate and authoritative information
with regard to the subject matter covered. It is sold with the understanding that
the publisher is not engaged in rendering legal, accounting, or other
professional advice. If legal advice or other expert assistance is required, the
services of a competent professional person should be sought.

—From a *Declaration of Principles* jointly adopted by a Committee of the
American Bar Association and a Committee of Publishers and Associations

Many of the designations used by manufacturers and sellers to distinguish
their products are claimed as trademarks. Where those designations appear
in this book and Adams Media was aware of a trademark claim, the
designations have been printed with initial capital letters.

This book is available at quantity discounts for bulk purchases.
For information, call 1-800-872-5627.

Dedication

This book is dedicated to Steve, who always cleans up after I'm through.

Acknowledgments

This book is the result of gifts given me by my many excellent teachers and friends and my happy association with the United States Marine Corps. But above all it is the result of my clients—wonderful, brave people who have shared their worlds with me and taught me what being human is all about.

Table of Contents

9: Communication and Anger / 177

The Art of Listening • Garble, Garble • The Story of Bruce and Sally • Nonverbal Communication • Proxemics • Lend Me Your Ear • Delivering Feedback • Three Blind Men and the Elephant • Self-Disclosure and Intimacy • Sending the Right Message • Blocks That Don't Build

10: It's Down to You: Assertiveness / 223

The Early Years • Styles of Interpersonal Behavior • Assertiveness Techniques

11: Conflict, Confrontation, and Those Nasty People / 245

What Is Conflict, Anyway? • Tricks of the Trade • Putting It All Together

Appendix: More Exercises / 259

Further Reading / 269

Index / 272

Introduction

An ice carver's artistry lies in her ability to envision something exquisite within the bulky parameters of a mundane block of ice and to know which tools will work best to achieve her goals. Similarly, a therapist working with people in trouble because of their anger, or because of domestic violence, or because of other pain-filled relationships, is faced with closed-down entities, brittle yet vulnerable. The therapist must consider and weigh, and at the same time chip away at, a system that's not working very well. The therapist has to whittle away at the structure of the client's anger system and the pain enclosed within.

In working with confused, unhappy individuals, couples, and families, I have gained new insight into anger, its sources and consequences, and I've had the opportunity to explore my ideas in my consulting practice and in teaching classes and workshops aimed at general audiences. What I have discovered has not only been of help to others but has allowed me to look at anger in new ways. This in turn has helped me discover that my ideas do not apply simply to anger and violence but also to all the other unhealthy stuff that anger brings with it.

When I asked clients who were initially angry, sometimes frightened (and sometimes frightening!), to describe what they were so mad about, they began to reveal new aspects of themselves. Rather than being the powerful, vengeful, in-control creatures they at first appeared to be, they began to reveal themselves to be actually pretty miserable people who felt out of control of their private universes.

Rather than being merely angry (the *Funk & Wagnall* definition of anger is "a feeling of sudden and strong displeasure and antagonism directed against the cause of an assumed wrong or injury"), they were *enraged*, not at one specific thing, but at everything at the same time. They described emotions that were overwhelming to them. It was almost as if they were trying to describe something out of Conrad's *Heart of Darkness,* where Kurtz exclaims the anguish in his soul: "The horror! The horror!"

How awful! How scary! How confusing! And, ultimately, how very sad for those who experience such anger.

After I had noted this difference between everyday garden-variety anger (the kind you get when someone cuts you off in traffic) and the almost mythic angst my clients were describing, it seemed important to look at this rage from different angles and determine how my clients came to feel so terribly powerless in its grip. In truth, when they allowed themselves to think about the way anger was ruling and ruining their lives, these folks felt awful about not only their behavior, but also about their feelings of helplessness.

To put it simply, they were scared! They viewed their rage as a self-perpetuating, continuous, all-powerful, and consequently hopeless condition. Over and over clients said that they felt stuck, that even the most insignificant things could feel so threatening that it was impossible to communicate their feelings. Many had almost given up— and no wonder! For some, this sense of threat and futility spilled over into all areas of their lives, and the result was even more frustration.

So, the question is, Were the intense feelings they were experiencing really feelings of anger, or were they something else? If they were something else, diagnosing them as having a "problem controlling their anger" and using typical anger management techniques (like time-outs) wouldn't really solve anything. In fact, it could easily add to their frustration level and ultimately make things worse.

While many books on anger touch on the idea of explaining what's beneath the anger response, most put forth anger management precepts in an almost confrontational fashion, from a didactic, or teacherly, power position. The common message has been, "What you're doing is wrong. Here's why. Now just shape up, or else."

In this book, I take a different approach. I help those who suffer from anger, or friends and loved ones of those who suffer from anger, to unravel their web of angst and seek positive solutions to their problem.

By looking at anger issues from a different angle, we can be kinder to ourselves and thus become better able to give ourselves reality checks without being defensive. When we are better able to explore our reactions without hostility and wariness, improved communication will result.

My hope is that, in evaluating the covered-up, subterranean emotions, you will gain the ability *to choose* how to react and develop improved problem-solving abilities that lead to safer, more productive solutions to anger. In this book, I will take a close look at anger, confrontation and conflict resolution, stress management, communication and assertion, and offer suggestions and exercises to help approach these problems in a positive, productive way.

You'll develop new skills that will enrich your life, and you'll gain the confidence to take charge and overcome your anger.

1

Anger's Terrain—
Keeping the Wolves
at Bay

Let's face it—if we didn't need anger, we probably wouldn't have evolved with it. Anger in itself is neither positive nor negative as an emotion—it is what you make it. It serves a function, though, and so it remains. Anger is very effective in accomplishing certain things. For instance, it helps us stay alive. Anger wakes us up. It arouses and gets us ready to take action. In the words of Mr. Spock from the TV series *Star Trek*, "Jim, madness has no purpose, no reason, but it may have a goal" (circa 1965).

Other species have instincts, those special little behavioral gizmos built right in that help them protect their interests when they are threatened. For example, big brown bears stand on their hind legs and bellow, tigers flatten their ears while exposing awesome choppers, bulls paw the ground, nostrils flaring, and even the wimpiest of dogs can snarl and yap like the dickens. In their own ways, these animals are trying to let you know they are a force to be reckoned with. They don't want to be messed with anymore. They look mad, growling and grimacing, but are they *angry*? They probably feel threatened about something, and their instincts are preparing them for what is termed the "flight or fight" response.

What we need to remember is that we behave as we do because of stuff that has been hard-wired into our brain's chemistry. We don't, after all, spend much time reminding ourselves to blink our eyes or hold our breath under water. These biological necessities are not that far removed from the same needs that "lower" animals exhibit in various overt ways, such as their behavioral displays of growling or snarling.

We, too, have incorporated certain behaviors into our makeup due to evolution. These behaviors may not be instincts, but they sure are good for keeping us alive! Unexpected situations demand quick responses. Clearly, in these situations, taking time to analyze motives may be detrimental to your health. (While you are sorting out your emotions, the lion may eat you or the mugger may shoot you!) So anything that can get you moving fast can foster the most primary of the biological urges, self-preservation.

But we humans no longer rely solely on instinct. As children develop, they gain what we call "impulse control"—the ability to control instinctual urges in favor of more socially acceptable behavior. Two-year-olds find out rather quickly in preschool that biting is unacceptable, and parents do their best to ignore the temper tantrums thrown by angry three-year-olds in hopes of extinguishing that behavior.

But what's an adult to do? Instead of biting, he's learned to substitute some behaviors for others and has evolved something loosely dubbed "anger" that accomplishes the same ends for him. After all, unless it's Hannibal Lector we're talking about, biting just isn't something that's expected from the average adult, but anger signals, such as yelling or glaring, might be considered acceptable.

As you probably recall from biology class, when man

3

(or woman) is faced with any of a myriad of threatening situations, this "anger" prepares him for the same survival-necessary "flight-or-fight" response that all other animals have. It clearly is some type of arousal state, but what state? And when we feel violated or threatened in some way, is the emotional experience always "anger," or is what we call "anger" merely a surface response to a perceived threat covering up more subtle (and scary) emotions underneath?

What Is Anger and Why Do We Get Angry?

You may wonder why I put the word "anger" in quotation marks. I set it off that way because I hope you might begin to consider looking at it in a new way.

Webster's dictionary tells us that anger is a term for "sudden violent displeasure or belligerence accompanied by an impulse to retaliate." That's fine as far as it goes, but couldn't "anger" also serve as a kind of a "temporary emotion"? Anger can allow us to protect ourselves from threat until we sort out the underlying emotion. That is to say, "anger" may be a kind of a handy catchall behavior that allows us to hold in or cover up other emotions that we can't understand or sort out at the moment.

The History of Anger

How and why does this anger response help us and when can it be appropriate? You can bet when our early ancestors came down from their trees and began trekking across the African savannah they had to develop some good survival skills in order to elude the much larger and even hairier predators of the time. Those old Australopithecus guys didn't have to think twice—their bodies' inherent survival mechanisms just kicked into gear and the fast ones lived see another day.

Similarly, when our Stone Age ancestors were faced with a threat, their hearts beat faster to pump more blood. Respiration increased to force oxygen into their lungs; digestion slowed to conserve needed energy. Those whose bodies responded and figured out clever evasive maneuvers lived to become our progenitors; those who didn't, didn't survive. Evolution just did the rest.

Later, in more hip, sophisticated Paleolithic times, many new survival strategies were added to our Cro-Magnon ancestors' "staying alive" tool pouch. Probably modeling the very creatures who threatened them, humans adopted some of the behaviors that they thought were most persuasive for asserting domination and a kind of "don't mess with me!" attitude.

Faced with salivating, starving wolves laying siege outside the dim and smelly cave containing his loved ones and, moreover, all of his food for the winter, our cave guy had better have come up with something that showed not only how tough he was, but more important, something that could psyche him up. He'd need something that would make him believe he was tough, something that forced him to take action for survival. (Plus, it was also not such a bad idea to act in a way that was intimidating to potential attackers.)

So what could he do? Get mad—really mad! So, our hairy guy gets a big, big club, grunts and hollers and makes ugly faces. Take that, you lousy wolves! And boy, did he feel better! Later, this type of display probably took on a ritual-like dimension. By performing the ritual, a kind of "magic" occurred that would give our hirsute hominid a sense of confidence.

5

And because (if it was successful) the performance of the ritual and subsequent action would be calming and self-soothing, it would be quite likely that he'd do the same thing the next time there were wolves at the door. It might even be tried with other predators—or family members. It thus became part of our cave guy's behavioral repertoire. (And this, of course, would have implications for subsequent generations of little cave persons to come.)

Anger in the Present Day

You can easily apply this scenario to the present day if you follow your ancestor's line of thinking—just plug in some of today's more modern strategies! Think, for instance, of the whooping and arm waving of the average football team (or their fans in the stands) and any of the menacing looks and gestures you undoubtedly have received if you drive on the highway. In these situations, modern man comes very close to the snarls of wolves and chest beating of jungle gorillas asserting their dominance.

Man's body automatically responds to threat (or perceived threat) in certain very measurable ways, ways that may be critical for survival under threatening circumstances. The body's muscles become tense, respiration increases, digestion stops, the heart pumps more blood to the brain in anticipation of quick action. However, *these ways can also become a threat to man if they are allowed to go unchecked in* unnecessary *situations.*

As was mentioned earlier, anger as an emotion is neither positive nor negative. It is merely a response to some type of stimulus. Perhaps because it does feel empowering, many people overuse anger as a self-preservation response. But, chronic reliance on anger can become a problem because it can be destructive to one's relationships as well as one's health.

If your anger or the anger of someone you love is negatively affecting your life, there is hope. Anger is usually a *temporary* condition, and it becomes a problem only if it becomes chronic or if you deal with it in destructive ways. The best news is that managing anger is not impossible once you gain insight into what kind of threat (or feeling of being threatened) causes it in you and how you react to it in self-defeating ways.

Remember—you have control over your anger. You get to decide what changes are necessary, and by reading this book, you will learn practical and positive ways to manage your particular anger style. A good way to start this process of change is by beginning to develop a sense of compassion, not only for others, but for yourself.

The Rules for Being Human

When you can give yourself and other people the benefit of the doubt, and when you can admit that it's not really even within your power to be perfect, you can begin to relax a little. You'll start focusing on finding new things to be happy about. As you become more forgiving of yourself and others, your anger resilience will grow.

Consider thinking about the following precepts.

1. You will receive a body. You may like it or hate it, but it will be yours for the entire period of this time around.
2. You will learn lessons. You are enrolled in a full-time informational school called Life. Each day in this

school you will have the opportunity to learn lessons. You may like the lessons or think them irrelevant and stupid.

3. There are no mistakes, only lessons. Growth is a process of trial and error: experimentation. The "failed" experiments are as much a part of the process as the experiment that ultimately "works."

4. A lesson is repeated until it is learned. A lesson will be presented to you in various forms until you have learned it. When you have learned it, you can go on to the next lesson.

5. Learning lessons does not end. There is no part of life that does not contain its lessons. If you are alive, there are lessons to be learned.

6. There is no better place than "here." When you're "there" has become a "here," you will simply obtain another "there" that will again look better than "here."

7. Others are merely mirrors of you. You cannot love or hate something about another person unless it reflects something you hate or love about yourself.

8. What you make of your life is up to you. You have all the tools and resources you need. What you do with them is up to you. The choice is up to you.

9. Your answers lie inside you. The answers to life's questions lie inside you. All you need to do is look, listen, and trust.

10. You will forget all this. You can remember it whenever you want.

—Anonymous

EXERCISE
Being Human

Think about a recent situation that made you angry and think about how you reacted to the situation. Ask yourself the following questions:

1. What need was I trying to meet with my behavior?

2. What pain or other feeling influenced my behavior?

3. What beliefs about the situation influenced my behavior?

4. While knowing I was responsible for my decision, no matter how unfortunate, can I accept that when I did it, I was only trying to survive?

5. I wish _____ hadn't happened, but it's over now. Can I let go of it and move forward?

6. Can I look at what happened as something I can learn from?

Remember, change and growth are possible!

Monkey See, Monkey Do

Cognitive therapists would argue (oops—*contend* might be a better word!) that anger and the other basic emotions—happiness, sadness, and fear—are at least partially based on a specific belief system that has been encoded in our brains that defines what's happening to us and how it is affecting us. Further, they would say that, based on their observations of human behavior, a person has a fair amount of control in deciding whether or not to become angry.

"Psshh," you say!

No, really! Think about a situation that made you really mad. Say for instance, you got angry because your neighbor not only left his garage door open (forcing you to have to look at the filthy interior), but also parked his car on the front lawn. Just where and when did you decide your neighbor's messy habits had anything to do with your angry feelings?

A lot of things that make us mad are things that are attached to how we grew up and the way in which our parents and society groomed us. It didn't even have to be something that was told or taught to us; it could have been something to which we were merely exposed. For example, a child who sees her sister burn her hand while trying to cook something on a stove will be leery of doing the same thing. She figures out that cooking can be a dangerous thing without actually experiencing a burn herself. We learn strategies for dealing with people in much the same way. We watch how other people do it, and we tend to follow their lead.

The teaching/learning situation can be either a single intense experience or it can be a learning that occurs from something witnessed frequently or learned over time. Think of the little kids you've seen who model their parents' behaviors, use the same mannerisms as their parents, or have the same vocal cadence as their parents when speaking. After all, it's what dress-up and pretend is all about: modeling and practicing to be just like Mommy or Daddy.

Not uncommonly, however, the behavior a child models loses something in the interpretation, and this can lead to problems. For instance, my daughter, at age three, put her kitty, Angel, into her toy Betty Crocker Easy Bake Oven. She closed the door and flipped the switch that safety-locked the door and turned on the oven. While this action was not exactly something she had modeled from me, it was a form of imitation nonetheless. She was cooking! The concept was okay—it was the execution (so to speak) that was the problem. (Angel did survive, one of her nine lives kaput no doubt, but only after I broke the oven getting the door open.)

The family is critically important and very, very powerful in teaching us the rules of correct behavior. That's okay as far as it goes, if the family is operating with reasonable rules. That is to say, a healthy family will have rules for behavior that are considered to be acceptable within the culture to which the family belongs. As long as there is no big family secret operating (like nobody knows that crazy Grandma is locked in the attic or that Dad beats the heck out of little brother Max), and as long as the family is neither too rigid nor too chaotic, it will receive reality checks from outside sources that keep it functioning well. The family system will model positive and healthy problem-solving strategies. But when a family uses outmoded or counterproductive strategies for problem solving, it is considered to be dysfunctional.

Family rules get passed down from generation to generation, so a dysfunctional family can lead to trouble. For example, when a child is exposed to a mom that goes ballistic when Dad doesn't listen to her and goes after him with her fingernails, the child may figure, that's life. Or when Dad takes off his belt and gives sister Mary a beating for mouthing off, a child may assume that's the way everybody handles their upsets. This stuff is usually not talked about outside the family. In fact, there may be strong interdictions against "airing the dirty laundry." As a consequence, the child doesn't have a chance to explore alternative behaviors. The family rules thus remain intact and unchallenged. These home-taught lessons can easily follow the child to school and translate into bullying or fighting with other kids or, worst-case scenario, even shooting at somebody.

The old TV series, *The Addams Family*, provides us with a rather far-out example of a family whose rules were definitely outside the norm. Everyone from Uncle Fester to Wednesday and Grand Mama happily subscribed to a set of family values that were downright bizarre. After all, most moms aren't vampires, and most kids don't play with guillotines. These kinds of behaviors may seem a little outside the ordinary to most, but because everyone in the Addams family went along with things as they were, the rules stayed intact. Even Lurch the butler (a pretty strange guy in his own way) went along with the family's unusual behavior.

The Message Is the Medium

How about *your* house when you were growing up? What kind of messages did you hear there? "Big boys don't cry"? "Good little girls should always say 'please' and 'thank you' and try to be nice"? "Think of the poor children (in wherever) and eat your food"?

Many of these parental edicts are probably popping into your head right now. All of them are filled with what cognitive psychologist Albert Ellis called "shoulds."

We all have our own personal lists of "shoulds" based upon our ages, cultures, and socioeconomic groups. This is not to suggest that internalized rules are always a bad thing. In order for a society or a culture (or a family) to exist, there needs to be some type of consensus regarding acceptable behavior, unacceptable behavior, and taboos (which are reserved for the most antisocial types of behavior). Many of these internalized rules become imbedded so deeply in our psychological makeup that we may actually be unaware of them. They are part of our personality structure.

As adults we tend operate on autopilot with some of these imbedded rules. And that's where trouble may be brewing. In relationships, even very simple differences in each partner's family rules can have damaging consequences. For example, newlyweds argue over whether or not the toilet seat should be left up or down. Couples make a big brouhaha over eating turkey or ham for Christmas dinner. And whether or not to open presents Christmas morning or the night before can lead to black eyes.

"Little" things and strongly held belief systems can mean quite a lot sometimes. Much conflict can arise in a relationship when a couple does not share common assumptions about even more important values. Making an assessment of the old "shoulds" that are still operating in our lives is the first important step in overcoming anger. Some of these "shoulds" may still be at work within us, and some may be harmless. I challenge you to make a list of your closely held ideas and beliefs that are operating in your own life.

Remember, keeping some of your "shoulds" operational is fine, so long as they don't cause you pain or problems in your life or relationships. For example, if somebody "should" be driving faster and it makes you so angry you run her into a ditch, or if your partner's views on politics make you so mad you get into a boxing match, then your belief system probably needs an overhaul. The information in this book will show you how to make positive changes in order to overcome your anger and prioritize your "shoulds."

Looking for Reality Checks

It's crucial when learning how to manage your anger and other emotions that you evaluate your "shoulds" and decide if they work for you or against you. Anger may be tied to the messages we got as children about what was "right" and "wrong" and "good" and "bad." Here's where a reality check might be helpful.

For instance, I once had a client, Sandy, whose life was negatively affected by her "shoulds." Sandy was a widow and had been dating a man for a year. Although she was clearly in love with him, she was unwilling to have a sexual relationship with him and it was causing problems between them. After a few sessions, we came to the root of her problem. She had been brought up to believe that good girls "should not" have sexual relations outside of marriage and she was not married to the guy! Sandy was a mature, unmarried woman, but for her, a rule was still a rule. And the rule was, good girls don't have sex outside of marriage. She had a dilemma.

At this point, Sandy was forced to look at this old familial "should" and consider whether it was still something that she could live with or whether it was time for her to unload it. Sandy's partner came in for a few sessions to discuss the situation. They decided to focus on building intimacy in the relationship in other ways and take the pressure off the sexual aspect for a time. Gradually, Sandy began to explore the idea of letting go of an outmoded belief system that was not appropriate in her present circumstances. Eventually, everything worked out satisfactorily for both partners!

The Identity Crisis, or Facing the Double Bind

Everyone comes to adulthood with his or her own personalized set of rules. Occasionally reviewing these rules can be helpful in allowing you to reevaluate their practicality and value in your current life situations. This exercise may help you decide to discard a few of your archaic nonfunctional precepts.

EXERCISE
What Are My Shoulds?

First, check out the list of "shoulds" below and see if you can identify with them!

1. I should never make a mistake.

2. I should always be polite.

3. I should always do whatever it takes to keep the peace.

4. I should always be smarter, more competent, or better than everyone else.

5. I should always think about the worst-case scenarios of a situation in order to be prepared.

6. I should always be cared for.

7. I should always feel loved and admired.

15

8. I should never say "no" to a loved one.

9. I should always be responsible for everything.

10. I should never be wrong.

11. I should never have to do something I don't want to do.

12. I should never have to wait for gratification.

Then, take a minute to write down the "shoulds" that *you* learned, implicitly and explicitly, in your family when you were growing up.

Next take a minute to write down the "shoulds" that prevail in your life now.

Compare your two lists. What has changed and what has stayed the same? Which "shoulds" from your childhood do you now realize were counterproductive? Are there any "shoulds" in your present-day repertoire that you believe might be wise to change or you could do without?

As children, we tend to believe that the stuff that our parents, teachers, and authority figures tell us is true. We're taught at an early age that if we follow the golden rule and other rules important to society, all will be well, so, as young children, we follow these rules without questioning. But by the time we reach our teenage years, we begin to see problems with this line of thinking. For the first time, we begin to question those values that were set forth to us. Perhaps Mom and Dad weren't right after all. We begin to see a new reality.

As emerging adults, recognizing this reality can be a frightening and disheartening thing. Despite the mantra of the golden rule, we may not always be treated with respect. We learn that promises can sometimes be broken, and we may find ourselves breaking promises to others. What we are actually feeling and what we believe we *should* be feeling may leave us with a sense of failure, confusion, and frustration, and these emotions don't feel good. They leave us feeling weak and helpless. As a result, we seek other outlets or strategies for dealing with our feelings. We may decide to deflect or project our vulnerable feelings on to somebody else, usually our parents and siblings, maybe even our friends. By doing this, we can then replace our "not good enough" feelings with a more powerful feeling—anger.

It's just plain easier to tell yourself that you're mad than it is to say you're sad, confused, hurt, or frightened. If you're sad, confused, hurt, or frightened, it's your problem—you must own it and take responsibility for it. However, if you're mad, you can blame others for the way you're feeling. Try going back through the anger to these kinder, gentler emotions. It is in facing them and learning how to deal with them that *you will overcome your anger.* Take a minute to look at what it was like as you were growing up.

EXERCISE
When I Was Little

Many of the things that took place in your family have had an impact on who you are now and what you believe about the world. Maybe you haven't thought about your childhood family in a while. Maybe now is a good time for a reality check.

Place a check mark next to any statements that apply to your childhood.

	Yes	No
At least one of my parents drank a lot or took drugs.	O	O
A lot of my basic needs were not taken care of.	O	O
My family was usually supportive of me.	O	O
You could never predict what would happen in my house.	O	O
I was ashamed of my family.	O	O
My family had lots of secrets.	O	O
I wasn't sure of the rules in my family.	O	O
Along with bad things, there were a lot of good things about my family.	O	O
I was always scared something bad might happen.	O	O
In my family there was open communication.	O	O
I had to take care of other people when I was young; I felt as if I was the parent.	O	O
I had a happy childhood.	O	O
My childhood is filled with wonderful memories.	O	O
I was beaten as a child.	O	O
It seemed as though there was never enough money to go around.	O	O
I never had any privacy.	O	O
My parent(s) were very distant/overinvolved.	O	O
I was sexually abused.	O	O

	Yes	No
I felt I could always understand the family rules.	○	○
I usually had a lot of fun with my family.	○	○
I'm proud of the family in which I grew up.	○	○
I felt isolated in my family.	○	○
I felt like my family cherished me.	○	○
I always felt my family accepted me for what I was.	○	○
I knew better than to talk about what went on in my family.	○	○
I really don't remember my childhood, but I sometimes think something really bad happened to me.	○	○
My friends were always welcome at my house.	○	○

Take a look at your answers. Did any of them make you feel happy? Did any of your answers disturb you in any way? Did any of them make you feel frightened, sad, anxious, or mad? Can you think about ways in which what happened to you as a kid are still influencing you today?

2

A Different Place or Time

People get angry for different reasons. Although anger is a universal feeling, its causes and expression can be culturally specific. What makes a Trobriand Islander mad is probably not going to tick off a New York City taxi driver, and the way each expresses his anger will be much different. The island guy would probably go nuts if you sawed through the stilts that supported his house. He might even try to put a curse on you.

A taxi driver couldn't care less, but cut him off in traffic and you'd hear some unusual epithets!

For example, a Marine once told me about a guy he knew in basic training. This young Marine had gone through extremely rigorous and nasty verbal abuse during boot camp at the hands of his Mephistophelian drill instructor. He had been insulted to the max and had been taken to the limits physically. He had not only withstood, but had succeeded fully in all the trials they could put to him. He was a stellar Marine. He was trained to handle the toughest physical and mental challenges out there. However, he went totally ballistic when the instructor called his mother an "old bag."

No doubt, he realized that the verbal haranguing and physical training he was undergoing was supposed to be honing him for his future job as a "devil dog." Clearly, this young man was reacting to one of the "shoulds" from his early childhood that told him mothers should not be insulted. He lost control and expressed his displeasure physically, resulting in the end of his military career. Whether you agree with that Marine's reaction or not, the only caveat here is to decide if the belief (and the reaction to the situation based on that belief) works to help achieve the desired results in the situation and within the context of the society. That's where the buck stops.

Sure, we may make some knee-jerk choices based upon our preordained hard-wiring, but, thanks to our brain's frontal lobe, these decisions are normally held in check by our assumptions regarding what we consider "reasonable." Sometimes this chain of consideration and action gets thrown out of whack and problems arise when individuals take action before they decide if their situation is threatening or if their response is appropriate. In addition, perceived threats in one society in terms of rules and values may not even warrant a flicker of consideration for folks from another culture.

Nature vs. Nurture

A lot of thought and rhetoric has gone into the debate over nature versus nurture. Researchers have squabbled for years over the answer. Are we built with our personalities already incorporated (nature), or did they develop as a direct result of the environment in which we were raised (nurture)?

Findings have shown that nature wins out over nurture. Early psychological experiments separated identical twins in order to determine whether different environments would result in different personality structures. Most of the studies indicated that regardless of the environments in which they were raised, the twins grew up with similar personalities. However, research did suggest that intelligence and other characteristics could be shaped and molded by the environment, or the nurture part of the equation.

Bottom line, our belief systems are influenced not only by our parents but also by our culture. But our personalities and our genetic predisposition mediate whether we will deal with anger by acting it out or by turning it inward and becoming depressed. Here is a fun and simple exercise to help you determine which of your personality traits are a result of nature or nurture.

EXERCISE
Nature vs. Nurture

1. *Nature:* Make a list of those aspects of your personality that you believe were genetically predetermined. Look at your parents and siblings. Think about their physical and mental similarities. Do you share any of these traits? What other aptitudes or talents do you share with your family? Once you figure out what you were born with, you can go on to explore what your culture and upbringing have contributed.

2. *Nurture:* Make a list of all the aspects of your personality you believe were molded by your early environment. Review your weekend rituals or the type of sports you played as a kid. Do you still enjoy doing the same things? Do you still participate in or enjoy watching the sports you learned as a kid?

While you cannot change the items in your "nature" category, you'll find by examining your list, there are probably at least a couple of things in your "nurture" category to which you can apply positive changes.

Exploring Your Anger Style

Everybody reacts differently when angry. Some people immediately let the world know they are mad. The storm clouds blow in fast and furious, the thunder roars, then the sunshine sparkles in the sky once again. Other people try to "suck it up" by minimizing their anger and putting on a happy face. These attempts at sublimation may work for a while, but the anger can ferment or escalate. In this case, the storm clouds get blacker and blacker until they just can't contain any more heaviness. The result is a huge downpour.

Do you know your anger style? To get a better idea, check out the three anger styles that follow.

Stuffers

"Stuffers" tend to deny their anger, minimizing it or keeping it in. They don't believe in their right to be angry. Stuffers often have these motivations:

- They fear offending people.
- They fear losing control.
- They fear losing a relationship.
- They are unable to cope with intense emotions.
- They believe their anger is inappropriate.

While the stuffer approach to anger management may stave off anger temporarily, eventually, the anger must be

25

released. As a result, the stuffer may wind up losing control, which can result in dangerous situations.

Escalators

"Escalators" blame the thing that provokes them, adding to already abusive situations. In an effort to feel okay, escalators look outside themselves to find a source for their upsets.

Escalators often have these motivations:

- They need to make their point.
- They try to use a different anger style than what they were raised with. (Perhaps they've been forcing themselves to be passive in a situation where they'd prefer to be more demonstrative in expressing their anger and finally the passive stance is no longer acceptable.)
- They need to be right.
- They need to get even.
- They frequently blame the other person or thing for making them angry.

Escalators can be dangerous. By escalating an already tense situation, they can provoke other people into responding to them with violence or can become violent themselves.

Managers

"Managers" use their anger to move themselves in a positive direction, unlike the stuffers and escalators. Using healthy strategies for dealing with their anger, managers see their discomfort as a call for change and finding solutions.

Managers often have these motivations:

- They allow themselves to have open discussion of the issues and remember to maintain their personal space and the space of the person with whom they are engaged.
- They stick to the topic at hand and don't drag in old stuff.
- They focus on behavior rather than the person themselves.
- They avoid blame and attack.
- They take responsibility for themselves and use their negative feelings as wake-up calls for change and growth.

Which of the three anger styles best describes your "anger profile"? In certain cases you may find yourself using one style or another, or maybe even combining a couple of them depending on the degree to which you feel threatened by a particular situation. Remember, your ultimate goal is to manage your anger in every situation possible. By paying close attention to the anger management style that you use most often and by incorporating the positive qualities of an anger manager into your actions, you'll find that your interactions will be more productive and you'll develop safer and more fulfilling relationships.

Gender Differences

As we have already noted, anger is a universal feeling. Without doubt, the norms and mores of society have a great effect on our conditioning and belief systems. But do these beliefs differ from gender to gender? Do females respond differently to anger than males?

Studies have shown that, even as little children, girls and boys tend to favor certain gender-based activities. While little girls use building blocks to fashion enclosures, little boys build towers. Given a choice, female children generally choose to play with dolls and little guys typically grab a truck. We know from this that boys and girls prefer doing different kinds of activities, but the question becomes, do they experience and express emotions, in particular anger, in different ways, too?

Men and women both receive many conflicting and unrealistic messages about anger. Boys receive early cultural prompts about what it means to be masculine. Being sensitive is great to an extent, but social conditioning says this can be "iffy," so let's not overdo it! Romantic comedy leading men like Jimmy Stewart and Cary Grant, whose style and gentle subtlety got them what they wanted, aren't around anymore. The present-day obsession with action films has made a cult of the "manly man." Unless he's playing for comedy, our hero has certain traditions to uphold. Clint Eastwood will never be found cowering under his covers! Sly is unlikely to run like a scaredy-cat and Jean-Claude would be damned if he couldn't kick his way out of a predicament. What's a guy to do?

Schwarzenegger has been able to make the transition from Conan to kindergarten cop, but he seems to be an exception. Most of the time, action-movie heroes send out the message saying in order to be a "real man," powerful and attractive to women, you have to be in control, tough and mean, and able to face danger, kill, maim, and generally devastate any opponent who crosses your path. Also, you must do it with not a hint of regret.

Football players may swipe one another on the fanny after a good play, but when knocked down on the field or near unconsciousness from broken parts, they do their best to maintain their composure, even if their tight manly grimace is one of pain. Marines, the guys at least, are taught to boast that they are trained killing machines. This attribute is naturally important during war and for maintaining good order and discipline, but a one-dimensional personality is not appropriate for every situation.

In our society, body language is mediated by rules that identify masculine and feminine behaviors. Many men are taught it's not a good thing to show softness or vulnerability or any of the other attributes of the "weaker" sex. Once boys learn how to hide their feelings, it's no wonder that admitting that they are weak, frustrated, confused, or frightened becomes abhorrent. Being angry just makes more sense! It just seems more "manly."

Boys continue to get the message from our culture that violent video games, violent sports, violent movies, violent rap music, and violent porno videos are all okay; that they're cool even! In fact, what they're hearing is they're wimps if they don't use violence in handling conflict. Hey, angry about your last math grade? Bring a gun to school. Show everybody just how mad you are! The tragedies played out in American high schools lately have served to focus our attention on the need to understand what's gone wrong with the message many young people have been hearing about how to handle their anger, and to begin to explore new ways for managing it.

Many women also receive conflicting messages about

how to handle anger. Frequently girls are taught that being angry is inappropriate and unacceptable. But angry feelings still exist and may be expressed verbally or with passive aggressive behaviors. Female clients have often talked about how they keyed their partner's car or slashed their husband's tires. When women exhaust other options for expressing anger, they can certainly become violent as well. Thelma and Louise obviously got fed up with a passive (or passive-aggressive) approach in dealing with their anger and frustration!

If you can buy into the idea that you are molded not only by nature but also by parental and cultural expectations and that your belief system plays a large role in how you interpret and respond to anger, you are well on your way to managing your feelings and your life in general. The first step is awareness.

Cultural Factors

Have you ever tried to drive in Europe or Asia? It can be a daunting experience for the uninitiated. Parisian customs and audacity can be frightening, and even walking across the streets in England can be dangerous. It's not that their ways are wrong, it's just that we're not used to the sporty, aggressive style of the French. And we're not used to having to look left then right when crossing the street. Americans can easily bump into people in England who are used to moving to the left when they pass on the street. We typically move to the right.

Other examples of cultural differences and spatial requirements come to mind. Anyone who has traveled in Europe or Asia has doubtless had the experience of waiting in seemingly endless lines. Queues, an honored tradition in England, where everyone waits, typically with patience, don't seem to exist in many other parts of the world. People just sort of smash in around each other in search of a point of vulnerability, like a wave flooding over a dike.

Generally speaking, in this country, people usually stay at arm's length. If they come any closer it is considered an invasion of our intimate space (a space reserved for little kids and lovers and such) and is considered to be angering because it is possibly physically threatening. This need for personal territory is different in every culture and maybe within individual families as well. There will be more about this in Chapter 9, where we discuss communication.

Threats to Body—Threats to Soul

Situations that threaten you physically are known as territorial threats. Whether we recognize it or not, we feel many territorial threats every day. From muggers on the street to terrorists to natural disasters, the feeling that we are being threatened can be quite valid!

For many people, however, abstract threats to their sense of self can be even more threatening and anger provoking than threats to their physical being. Things that threaten self-esteem and self-efficacy (threats to a person's perceived ability to manage himself or his surroundings effectively) are for many, more devastating than physical threats and prompt much more severe reactions. By constantly berating yourself and feeling as though you've screwed up or that you are a worthless person, you become a threat to your own self-esteem.

Can you identify what you perceive as threats to your body and threats to your soul? Take a few minutes to do the following exercise and find out how you perceive threats and what angers you most.

EXERCISE
Identifying Threats

For each of the following items, decide whether it presents a physical threat (territory) or an emotional threat (self-esteem). Then rate each one from 1 to 5, with 5 being something that provokes the most anger in you, and 1 being something that provokes very little or no anger.

1. You lend your car to a friend with a full tank of gas. He returns it to you with a nearly empty tank and says nothing about compensating you.
   Territory   **Self-Esteem**   **Rating**
   ○   ⦿   _2_

2. You are stood-up for a date.
   Territory   **Self-Esteem**   **Rating**
   ○   ⦿   _2_

3. You are going to pick up a friend and are forced to wait while a freight train goes by.
   Territory   **Self-Esteem**   **Rating**
   ⦿   ○   _4_

4. You're trying to nap at the beach. Noisy children wake you.
   Territory   **Self-Esteem**   **Rating**
   ⦿   ○   _1_

5. You'd like to state your opinion, but no one will listen.

Territory	Self-Esteem	Rating
○	⊘	_3_

6. You're in the middle of a dispute and your adversary calls you a jerk.

Territory	Self-Esteem	Rating
○	⊘	_4_

7. You're working on a report and your hard drive crashes.

Territory	Self-Esteem	Rating
⊘	○	_3_

8. Somebody keys your car.

Territory	Self-Esteem	Rating
⊘	○	_2_

9. You get slapped in the face.

Territory	Self-Esteem	Rating
○	⊘	_4_

10. The waitress brings you cold soup.

Territory	Self-Esteem	Rating
⊘	○	_1_

11. Someone criticizes you in front of others.

Territory	Self-Esteem	Rating
○	⊘	_4_

12. Someone spits at you.

Territory	Self-Esteem	Rating
○	⊘	_4_

13. Someone makes fun of your spouse.

Territory	Self-Esteem	Rating
⊘	○	_2_

14. You accidentally bang your shin on a chair.

Territory	Self-Esteem	Rating
◙	○	1

15. You lose a game.

Territory	Self-Esteem	Rating
⊕	○	1

16. You need to get someplace in a hurry, but the car in front of you is doing 20 mph and you can't pass.

Territory	Self-Esteem	Rating
⊕	○	3

17. Your employer tells you your work is lousy.

Territory	Self-Esteem	Rating
○	⊘	3

18. You discover someone deliberately sold you something defective.

Territory	Self-Esteem	Rating
⊕	○	2

19. Someone is talking about you behind your back.

Territory	Self-Esteem	Rating
○	⊘	3

20. You step on a wad of gum.

Territory	Self-Esteem	Rating
⊗	○	1

21. A repairman overcharges you.

Territory	Self-Esteem	Rating
⊘	○	2

22. Everybody on the freeway around you is doing 75 mph, but the cop comes after you.

Territory	Self-Esteem	Rating
⊗	○	_1_

23. Someone tells you to "go to hell."

Territory	Self-Esteem	Rating
○	⊗	_3_

24. Someone cuts you off in traffic; you swerve and nearly hit another car.

Territory	Self-Esteem	Rating
⊗	○	_1_

25. Your spouse is three hours late getting home and doesn't bother to call you.

Territory	Self-Esteem	Rating
⊗	○	_2_

> **Score yourself:**
> **Self-esteem items** _32_
> **Territorial items** _19_

Generally speaking, in what kinds of situations do you feel more vulnerable? In order to accurately assess and overcome your anger, you must learn to make the distinction. Do you find yourself bothered more by situations that can physically harm you or by situations that are potentially damaging to your self-esteem?

Did you find that you scored higher in items that dealt with territorial threats or in situations that threatened your sense of self-efficacy? If you're like many people, you may be surprised to discover that occurrences that you perceive to be robbing you of your esteem can be extremely threatening and anger provoking.

We don't have the power to change things like earthquakes and hurricanes. But we do have the power to change how we think about ourselves, the way people see us, and the way in which we operate in the world. Rather than simply being a "reactor," responding to things that happen in your life, you become a "designer" when you become more of aware of your behavior and your attitudes. This awareness will supply you with more control in creating situations that are favorable and safe.

Strategize for Survival

As you look over your answers in the previous exercise, try to discern particular relationships, issues, and even times of day that can lead to trouble. For instance: You may know that taking a certain route home after work usually makes you crazy due to the amount of traffic or the road conditions at a certain time of year. Do you continue to take that route when there is another route that might be a little longer, but a lot less stressful for you? Or, you may know that your mother-in-law (who you can't stand) typically calls to talk with your spouse at a certain time every day. Do you answer the phone anyway? You have the power to deal with these issues in a more positive way.

As you get to know your anger style, you will be able to discern where certain types of situations fall on your own personal continuum of distress. Exploring what kind of discomfort you experience when you're angry can help you prevent knee-jerk reactions. In becoming more familiar with your anger style, you will also be able to strategize how to avoid certain situations. While it is impossible to avoid all troubling situations, using discretionary power in your own behavior management repertoire can be seen as a form of assertion—*it demonstrates that you are taking charge of getting your own legitimate needs met in a way that is not destructive to you or others.*

The good news is, the more you manage to get your needs met in positive ways, the more your sense of mastery will grow. Even if you cannot avoid anger-causing situations, you can still use your new insights into what makes you angry—and why—to control how you react to these situations. Still more good news is that anger is usually a *temporary* condition and it becomes a problem only if it becomes chronic or if you deal with it in destructive ways. The best news is that managing anger is not impossible once you gain insight into what kind of threat (or feeling of being threatened) causes it in you and how you react to it in self-defeating ways.

Deciding to Change

Even though changing your behavior may lead to a more satisfying life, it can be a tough decision to make. When you make a commitment to change, you risk losing what's familiar to you. Your relationships and sense of identity may change, too. Old coping patterns will be called into question. So it's no wonder part of you may be ready to change while another part of you may resist. Be gentle with yourself and remember that change is a process—it doesn't happen all at once.

There are a few things you should become aware of as you get ready to begin to change. First, you must believe that a change would be a good thing. Maybe you've been more conscious lately of how others are reacting to you or how you are feeling about yourself. Perhaps you have become aware of the fact that your life is filled with confrontation. (See, you're already there!)

Next comes the step where you think about how you might go about making the necessary changes. This step requires some self-scrutiny and honest self-assessment. Perhaps things don't feel as safe as they once did or perhaps all the anger is having a detrimental effect on the quality of your life or your family's life. Perhaps you are having legal problems.

The next step is making the preparations to change. This is the step where commitment comes in, where you affirm that change is possible.

After that you come to the part of the process where you take action.

Lastly, in order for the change to take effect and stay in force, there must be a mechanism for maintenance. That means practice! (By reading this book, you have taken action, and by doing the exercises, you will be supplied with some of the practice you need for maintenance.)

As you think about changing your behavior, it's helpful to look at what you face. *Your life may become different, but you can be ready for the changes.* Take a few minutes to think about what parts of your life may change as you do. Then complete the following exercise.

EXERCISE
Deciding to Change

If you do decide to change and grow, how will the following probably be different?

Write your answers. Then place a check mark next to things you see as positive and two checks next to those you see as negative.

In my work:

_____

_____

In my relationship with my partner:

_____ *much better* _____

_____

In my lifestyle:

_____

_____

Inside myself:

_____ *|'* _____

_____

With my kids:

_____

_____

Other things that might change:

_____

_____

Now try this one:

What would I have to give up if I change?

Control

What am I most afraid to give up?

What seems easy to give up?

Do I have specific fears in regard to changing my behaviors?

What surprised me most about my responses?

How'd you do?

3

Do I Feel?

How many of us acknowledge our feelings? We think about how we feel, sure. We have mental conversations like, "Oh, jeez, my hairline is starting to look like my father's," or "I'm acting just like my mother." We continually bombard ourselves with negative thoughts like, "I just know that guy is checking me out. I wonder if he thinks I'm too fat." But that's all *thinking* stuff.

How often do we actually stop to consider what is causing these negative thoughts? How often do we acknowledge our unmet needs and fears? How often do we really understand why we feel angry? Until we are clear what motivation lies behind our thoughts, how can we be sure that our needs are being met? Try the next exercise to find out how you handle your feelings.

EXERCISE
How Do I Handle My Feelings?

Think of something that made you happy or mad and ask yourself the following questions about the situation.

1. Was I aware that I was feeling something?

2. Can I assign a name to what I was feeling?

3. Can I now agree that I had the right to this feeling? Was what I felt legitimate?

4. Can I acknowledge that how I felt might have come not only from the present circumstances, but also from something that happened in the past?

5. Did I have the appropriate reaction or take the appropriate action?

Here's an example of how these underlying emotions can have an effect on us. "LeAnn" came for a consultation because she was extremely angry. Her husband "Dan" had left the front door open when he went out to the store and left her alone for a few minutes. Nothing unusual happened while he was out, but when LeAnn discovered he'd left the door ajar, she went ballistic. When he returned home, she started a huge fight with Dan, ranting that he was inconsiderate and didn't care about her. During the therapy session, she said she felt as though she had overreacted, but she just couldn't stop being mad at him— didn't want to be near him, in fact—and she couldn't figure out why.

I asked LeAnn to name the feelings behind the anger she was feeling and what needs were affected? Was it her need for physical safety that was threatened, or did what happened challenge her sense of self in some other way? Did her husband's action evoke some anxiety-creating feeling from her distant or near past? Did her reaction make sense? Was her reaction appropriate to the situation in kind and intensity? Lastly, I asked LeAnn to look at how she was feeling about what happened and whether or not her feelings about the situation changed since then?

It turned out that LeAnn remembered that when she was a little girl, her dad had left her home alone and an intruder had gotten into the house. She was smart enough to hide in a closet while her house was ransacked. Even though she was okay, she carried that memory of vulnerability and fear with her. Her frightening emotions translated into anger at her father that, at the time, she was not allowed to explore. Those were the emotions she transferred to Dan. Dan just got the brunt of LeAnn's childhood anger and fear. Tracking her underlying feelings back to their origin allowed LeAnn to look at the current problem in a new way. She was able to let go of her anger at her husband. She was further able to explain to Dan why she was behaving in what appeared to be an unreasonable way and ask that he be more careful about closing the door in the future.

Trying to determine your layers of feelings can be tough. Think about a situation that made you angry and then complete the following exercise. This exercise will help you make strides toward identifying and controlling your anger.

EXERCISE
Identifying and Controlling My Anger

Why did I get angry?

_____

_____

At the time, how did I interpret what the other person did to me?

_____

How did I feel about it at the time?

humiliated

What kind of threat did I feel (physical, self-esteem, etc.) or what need did I fear I would be prevented from satisfying?

Self-esteem

Looking back on it now, was my interpretation of the situation accurate and rational?   **Yes / No**
If "no," why not?

Was my reaction to the perceived threat appropriate?   **Yes / No**
If "no," what would have been a better way to react to the situation?

How can I avoid reacting in an inaccurate, irrational, or inappropriate way in the future?

By using this exercise to analyze your past perceptions and reactions to threatening situations, you can come to a new understanding of your reactions to such situations. Use the exercise each time you encounter a situation that angers you to help you understand your layers of feelings as you work toward healthier anger-management skills.

Learning the ABCs—Only You Can Make You Angry

Psychological research has shown that it's not so much what happens to you in life, but the way you look at it that largely determines your satisfaction and happiness. Now this may sound a little sugarcoated to you, but it is largely true. There will always be situations that threaten you physically or emotionally, making you angry. However, with time and effort, you will learn that many situations you perceive as angering at first can be reframed using safer constructs. We can do some pretty amazing things with our belief systems—for good or for ill.

Originally, psychologists believed that we experienced emotions as the consequences of events. This relationship was viewed as causal—as things happened to us, we reacted with some type of feeling or emotion. Now it is widely believed that there is a whole lot more to emotional reactions. Look at it this way. Say, for instance, that (1) *something* happens to you, but even before you feel something, you have a (2) *thought* about that something that happened. A nanosecond later you establish some (3) *belief* about what happened. And it's only after you have evaluated the event according to your belief system that you have a (4) *consequent emotion* about what has occurred. Your belief system acts as a kind of filter through which all information about the world has to pass.

In this way of thinking, the *belief* stage becomes critical in determining how you perceive (and feel about) your universe. It follows that you have to accept most of the responsibility for determining the emotional outcomes of your interactions. In many circumstances, you have the say over how you are going to react, based upon your beliefs regarding the event.

When you can check yourself for irrational beliefs, you can change your tired ways of thinking and dump the wind out of the sails of your anger boat. In other words, *only you can make you angry.*

Personal Responsibility

Acknowledging that you are in charge of your emotional life is a great first step. In order to continue on the path to overcoming your anger, there are other types of anger-related behavior that you must understand.

When you're in pain, you tend to blame others. Pinning your blame on someone else allows you to feel justified in your anger. Once freed from responsibility for your problems by placing blame elsewhere, you can wallow in self-pity. By choosing to wallow, you give up your power and get only resentment in return. Anger costs too much. However, by accepting personal responsibility for your problems, you are empowered to try new strategies in order to satisfy your needs.

Maybe you can imagine a situation like this one. Say you've been feeling overwhelmed at work and that you believe your boss hasn't been giving you the credit you deserve. Remember, you have a choice about your reaction to this situation:

- **Negative:** You're angry and hurt, but you figure that you can't do anything about how you're feeling so you suck it up and try to keep your feelings to yourself. That's not a very satisfying thing to do, so to get even, maybe you sabotage a project or two and eventually you get fired.

- **Positive:** You decide to approach your employer and explain how you're feeling about things. Your boss can, of course, then ignore your input, but perhaps she'll do something that makes you feel better, who knows? In this scenario you may at least have a chance of getting your needs met.

You decide which solution is in your best interest.

Hot Thoughts

Hot thoughts are subconscious negative thoughts that may influence the way we perceive a situation. Hot thoughts can work for you or against you, depending on the situation. For instance, if you've been having some hard times, these subtle (or maybe not so subtle) thoughts may take the form of put-downs and "not good enough" messages.

You can learn to identify some of your own internal "hot talk." By taking note of your personal themes, you can begin to stop your negative thoughts and replace them with healthier, more self-affirming blandishments. In doing so, you will improve your self-image and become better at managing your reaction to anger-provoking situations. Some of the most common hot thoughts are listed in the next section and will be explored further in Chapter 8.

Types of Hot Thoughts

There are a few classic types of hot thoughts that you may be using when you get angry. You also may be using these in your self-talk or in your interactions with others.

Labeling

When you label, or pigeonhole, the source of your anger, it becomes easier to rage over. Once you've smacked a "bad" label on something, you've decided how you feel about it—no ifs, ands, or buts—and it is no longer necessary for you to analyze, interpret, or understand it. If you allow yourself to see things as only black and white, then it becomes easier to escalate your anger.

When possible, try to avoid black-and-white thinking. Try not to decide that things are either *all good* or *all bad*, *all right* or *all wrong*. Look for shades of gray. That goes for labeling people as well. It's all too easy for us when you feel wronged by someone to slap a label on that person based on his or her conduct. Generally, it's what a person is *doing* that causes you grief, but you wind up labeling the *person* a "jerk" or a "racist" or a "slob." Classifying someone in this way makes it easier to see the whole person as despicable and therefore more deserving of your anger.

Mind Reading

Mind readers believe that by reading subtle signs they can discern what's going on in other people's—especially their partners'—minds. (This type of interpretation goes beyond the ability to understand nonverbal communication or body language.) A woman who believes she can read minds may incorrectly attribute this skill to her partner, too, and then become incensed when her mate behaves as though he doesn't have "the sight."

Here's an example of how believing in mind reading can lead to problems. "John" came to therapy to work on his relationship. He was frustrated and wanted to know why it was that when his wife was upset, she thought he should be able to feel it and should be able to anticipate her needs and give her a hug or take her out or buy her something. He said that eventually his wife would let him know what she wanted from him and he'd comply, but his efforts never seemed good enough for her. He felt his wife seemed to think he should *know in advance* what was needed. I was guilty of this, myself—I confess. When I was upset, I just *knew* that my husband should feel it, that he should, in fact, *anticipate* it and give me a hug. But as I have been trained to know better, to understand that only *I* can get my needs met, I go ahead and ask for the hug. He complies. (He's a nice man.)

Fortune-Telling

Somewhat akin to mind reading, fortune-telling is based upon supposed "knowledge" of what is happening in someone else's life. Fortune-tellers behave according to what they believe will happen and not according to the actual reality of the situation. They act on assumptions that haven't been verified. The next example is based on an actual situation in which fortune-telling caused a misunderstanding.

"Jennifer" got into a pique and decided to throw out the lavish dinner she made for her husband because he was twenty minutes late for dinner. She immediately assumed the worst, guessing that he had gone to a bar with his friends and wouldn't come home until very late. In a rage, she dumped the entire dinner into the garbage disposal. Jennifer's husband came home shortly thereafter—he had been stuck in traffic with no cell phone. Despite her mistake, she ranted at him in an attempt to justify her behavior based on her false projection regarding his actions. Jennifer's husband was in a no-win situation.

Obviously, this type of thinking can be quite disastrous. Communication is squelched. Fortune-telling leads to more and more dysfunctional communication because it compounds misunderstanding. Utilizing his or her erroneous belief system, each party gets farther and farther away from knowing what is really going on.

Catastrophizing

Catastrophizing occurs when someone takes a rather mundane occurrence and blows it out of proportion. Looking at situations from the perspective that they are truly awful can crank up your sense of victimization (and importance), making you feel deeply wronged. This type of hot thought may be somewhat gender specific—specific to women, that is. Here's why: When women describe things, they tend to use more superlatives and grander language than men do. It's probably just a matter of style. For example, "I have the most horrible headache. I think I may die," or "You never want to kiss me anymore, I guess you hate me," and so on.

This type of intensity simply confounds men. The facts just don't fit! Stunned by such statements, men frequently fail to react appropriately, if at all. Women can all too easily interpret men's state of bewilderment as a lack of commitment or caring. This conclusion further contaminates the system of communication while giving neither participant a clue as to what the other person needs. This perceived disregard for the other's needs often leads to a lack of satisfaction with the relationship and, not surprisingly, big problems. However, regardless of your gender, avoiding exaggeration as much as you can and working on being more direct will help improve communication with the people you must interact with every day, be it family, friends, or coworkers.

Shoulding

Watch out for shoulding on yourself—you know, phrases like, "I should have known better," or "I should be thinner," or "I should have gotten new tires on the car and I wouldn't have gotten in the accident." Such self-punitive "should" statements can be very demoralizing and serve only to exacerbate guilt and fire up self-anger. Look at these shoulds squarely, see if there is any reality in any of them, and refute the rest if you can. If somebody else is shoulding on you, short circuit your anger with inquiry. Ask the other person what it's all about. Remember, you'll stay angry just as long as you accept the truth of any angry belief.

Distorted Thinking Patterns

In addition to being hot thoughts, shoulds can also cause you to operate under a system of wrong or negative thinking that contributes to self-angering. Try the next exercise and begin to get rid of some of the unnecessary shoulds in your life. Spend a little time to think through your answers.

EXERCISE
Getting Rid of My Shoulds

What irrational should do I want to dispute and then surrender?

_____

_____

Can I rationally support this belief in my present circumstances?

_____

_____

What evidence exists of the falseness of this belief?

_____

_____

Does any evidence exist of the truth of this belief?

_____

_____

What are the worst things that could happen to me if I did not believe this or I did not get what I believed I must have?

_____

_____

What good things could happen if I no longer held this belief?

_____

_____

Many of our negative interpretations are rather arbitrary at best. They are ideas assigned at some time in the past but which no longer apply. By deciding if such beliefs are still influential in your life and refuting and then discarding those that are unnecessary, you go a long way toward managing, rather than being managed by, your emotions. Once you accomplish this, you will be able to focus on developing your ability to communicate assertively. (Managing your emotions is covered in Chapter 5, and learning communications skills is covered in Chapter 9.)

If you don't cast out unnecessary shoulds, it's easy to fall prey to negative patterns of thinking. There are five negative patterns of thinking that you should try to identify within yourself.

Personalization

Teenagers are especially prone to this negative thought pattern. My teenage daughter, for example, exhibited personalization on a regular basis. She was convinced that people were looking at her "funny." She was sure that the entire world was just waiting to ogle her or label her in some way—fat, thin, weird, the list goes on and on. She had fallen prey to personalization, which means incorrectly referring external events to herself. She was the victim of a wacky solipsism, so self-absorbed (like most kids at that age) that everything was all about her.

Polarized Thinking

Simply put, this is dichotomous either/or thinking, often setting up conditions for an assumption. In its way, polarized thinking seems logical. It is the *premise* that's the problem. Here's an example: "If my husband really loved me, he wouldn't come home late for dinner. He's late, so he must not love me." The problem is that one part of the syllogism is defective to begin with. That is to say, coming home late does not necessarily prove a lack of loving.

Inference

A kissing cousin to polarized thinking, inference is a kind of distortion that's even more far out. Inference usually consists of jumping to an arbitrary conclusion in the absence of any corroborating evidence. For example, thinking, "George didn't smile at me today when he came to work. He always smiles at me. He must have gotten fired and he probably thinks it's because of me." When you catch yourself thinking in this way, it's best to stop and check yourself for inconsistencies in your logic.

Selective Abstraction

Selective abstraction is a very common distortion between couples. It occurs when you focus on a detail while ignoring the context in which it is occurring. Say, for example, "Betty" dresses to go out to dinner with her husband and thinks she looks pretty darned good. She says to her husband, "How do I look?" He smiles and says, "Good, but you have a run in your stocking." She goes nuts. This isn't what she wanted to hear. Her husband was just stating the facts, being helpful, but that doesn't matter: Now she doesn't even want to go out anymore. "Betty" has succumbed to selective abstraction.

Overgeneralization

Overgeneralization means arriving at some sweeping conclusion based on a single experience, particularly if you've had a bad day. For example, resolving never to drive again after getting into a small fender bender is an overgeneralization. In every conflict, you have the task of communicating your needs and trying to understand the other person's point of view, even if the two of you don't agree. Chapter 9 on communicating will provide you with more communication tools to better deal with these types of distorted thinking patterns.

Fight the Good Fight

Life is a two-way street. People are constantly evaluating you, just as you are constantly evaluating them. Your appraisal of them may be based upon several things: how a person looks or smells, what kind of car the person drives, how much money he has, or how she is dressed. Any negative or positive assessments are based upon your own set of rules about how others should behave and under what circumstances.

However, assuming that other people are working with the same set of rules that you are can lead to incorrect interpretations and conclusions. Instead of assuming, try to look at *why* the other person acts in the way that he or she does and understand that his or her rules may be different from yours. The more you understand the *conceptual* and *experiential framework* and *assumptions* under which others act, the better you will be able to understand where someone is coming from.

Of course, just because you understand the reasons for another person's behavior doesn't mean that you will approve of it or that it will be acceptable to you. However, as you analyze that person's behavior, you can learn to see it in a more objective cause-and-effect framework. This enhanced perspective not only helps you to regulate your own reaction to the interaction, but also even helps you attain greater mastery over the situation.

As Don Miguel Ruiz reminds us in his book, *The Four Agreements* (Marin County, CA: Amber-Allen Publishing, 1997), "Nothing others do is because of you. What others do is a projection of their own reality, their own dream. When you are immune to the opinions and actions of others, you won't be the victim of needless suffering." Sometimes we get caught up in entitlement fallacy—the belief that just because we want something very much or just because we believe we need something very much, we ought to have it and *anyone who gets in our way is doing it on purpose!* This kind of belief is quite normal for three-year-olds—it's a normal stage of ego development. But for an adult, it's a reaction that must be laid to rest.

Believing in the entitlement fallacy can lead to self-angering thoughts and behaviors. For example, you might have thought, *if* my girlfriend loved me, she'd answer her phone by the third ring. She didn't, so evidently she doesn't love me anymore or she's out screwing around. Just because you want something to be a certain way doesn't mean it will be. We need to recognize this fact and not give some funky belief the power to make us mad.

Anger Management Tools for Dealing with Others

In your relationships with others, viewing anger in someone else as a response to some type of personal pain will help you to take your own feelings out of the situation. In focusing on the other person, you have a better chance of getting a clear, nondefensive picture of what the person needs. You may even be able to provide it and thus avert an escalating anger situation. Try to begin to use the following tools in your interactions with people, and watch your anger mastery skill grow.

1. **Inquiry is a good management tool for you to practice.** Be sure to ask questions of the other person

57

about the potentially angering situation. Inquiry helps your communication skills, and it can deescalate potentially volatile situations while at the same time allowing you to make note of your own responses to anger-provoking situations. Asking questions helps you evaluate your ability to accept personal responsibility for your feelings. Things may not be as they seem and there may actually be no real cause for anger. For instance, if someone storms into the room, try not to immediately become defensive and assume he is angry because of something you did. Ask; he might just be having a lousy day.

2. **Take responsibility.** Make sure you are responsible for your own actions. Blaming others just makes things worse as you set up a system for yourself of labeling others in negative ways. Ultimately, blaming others is counterproductive. The person being blamed will eventually give up trying to meet any positive expectations you may have, believing it's probably impossible to do so. Being eternally damned as an idiot or a failure, this person doesn't stand a chance.

3. **Become aware of your body.** Scan your body for stress. Physical tension creates stress and *stress predisposes you to anger.* Because anger shows up somatically, patients in therapy are taught to survey themselves for evidence that their bodies are showing clues of discomfort, which can lead to anger. They learn to recognize where they carry tension in their bodies. A twitching jaw, a changed breathing pattern, a hard-beating heart can all be indicators that your body knows, maybe even before

you are consciously aware of it, that you're experiencing discomfort. Look for some of these anger clues in yourself. By taking on the role of aware self-observer, you can gain a bit of objective distance, which will give you more time to decide how you wish to respond in the situation.

4. **Stay on track.** You don't need to let provocation get the better of you. If somebody provokes you by bringing in old material, ignore it and stay in the here and now. Try not to get your anger hackles up, thinking about how you've been wronged in past situations. Give yourself the basic message that you are in charge and that you *do* have the skills to manage most every situation. Supply yourself with good healthy self-talk and watch your esteem grow.

4

Anger and Family Violence

It probably doesn't come as a big surprise that individuals and families who are suffering from problems with anger may share many of the same dynamics with other families in which violence occurs. Anger can manifest itself as abuse against one's partner or one's children. It may take the form of verbal or mental abuse or neglect or may segue into the realm of physical or sexual violence. In the United States, the incidents of violence that occur against a spouse, boyfriend, former boyfriend, girlfriend, or former girlfriend are estimated to range from a little under one million to three million each year. Violence is certainly not uncommon, but just because there are anger problems, doesn't mean that violence will always follow. However, both violent and nonviolent families may have a few dynamics in common.

So it can be helpful in understanding and overcoming your anger for you to explore how the two situations are connected and why this may be the case. Anger, rage, and ultimately violence are all part of a continuum of behavior. This behavior can range anywhere from the threatening glower or the angry word, to actual physical assault or assault with a deadly weapon. It's all a matter of degree. The question is, how do these behaviors relate to one another and how did these behaviors come about to begin with?

Down Through the Ages—A Quick Trip Through Time

Violence has been around for as long as humankind has been in existence. Perhaps you remember our cave guy and all the ideas he came up with for protecting his cave family and keeping them in line? Power and control have been important dynamics for most societies from the get go and, no doubt, the use of threatening behaviors, coercion, and violence helped things along. They helped get the message across about who had the power and provided a nice setup for punitive action if someone didn't happen to agree. All these behaviors had to do, once again, with social learning theory.

Even in the earliest times and even in the female-controlled matrilineal societies, violence was used at least in ritual form. In many of the early Indo-European agricultural societies, a male would be chosen as the representative of a god, a corn-god perhaps. Or perhaps he would represent some other potent deity. He would be wined and dined, entertained *big time* by the queen, and pampered by the tribe, and at the end of his appointed term as "the god," he would be ritually sacrificed. He would be slaughtered as a means of demonstrating obeisance to the earth goddess in order to bring about the earth's fertility.

Later, as the guys took over and more patriarchal societies began to develop, women took on the more subordinate role. They were considered to be a man's property and were, therefore, easily disposed of. In many societies they accompanied their husbands to the afterworld, kicking and screaming maybe, but, hey, it was the way things were done. Whether it was on a burning boat or some other type

63

of pyre really didn't matter much—they were still goners. The strong dominated the weak, and aggression, power, and control were, after all, the tenets upon which the world operated.

Obviously, the idea of people as property has been with us down through the years and has revealed itself under many different guises. The application of the principle can be applied not only to the "battle of the sexes," but also to other groups as well. Entire civilizations sought to dominate less favored ones. Proponents of different religions sought to overcome whoever was considered to be "heathen" of the day. These themes occur over and over throughout history and are, quite obviously, still occurring today. People have always wanted to dominate others for reasons that are religious, political, territorial, and cultural, or by some other motives or unidentified needs. The fact remains that, within the family, someone's need to dominate, to control, or to overpower can lead to big problems.

A Good Rule of Thumb and Other Big Ideas

Have you ever heard the expression "That's a good rule of thumb"? It's an expression that comes down to us from English common law. This law conferred upon a husband a legal right to keep his wife in line. He was encouraged—even admonished—to use a rod on her in order to correct any "wrong" behavior. The only stipulation was that he could use a rod no thicker than his thumb for this purpose. Pity the woman whose hubby had really big hands. Men with small thumbs were probably much sought after as husband material in the sixteenth and seventeenth centuries!

Time moved on and what went on behind closed doors remained the personal business of the family. Power and control continued to be the mainstay of most Western societies. The Spanish Inquisition and the Salem witch trials inflicted pain and suffering on anybody who didn't fit in with the status quo. Various countries who engaged in empire-building schemes, and a plethora of territorial and religious wars, saw to it that the doctrine of "might makes right" continued to flourish. Darwin showed up in the nineteenth century and told us all about that cool concept "the survival of the fittest." The ball just kept on rolling.

The Twenty-First Century Update

Although without doubt wars were, and of course still are, in vogue, in the beginning of the twentieth century questions began to arise as to the legitimacy of using power tactics within the family. It was considered to be the norm in most families for Dad to be the boss. Dad was top dog, and then came Mom. Marriage ceremonies, many Christian ones anyway, had set it up, after all, so the woman agreed to love, honor and *obey* her husband. The kids were at the bottom of the heap with even less say than Mom. It was pretty much an accepted fact that Dad was king of the castle. Most families were not democracies. But certain other segments of the population had begun to wonder about whether this plan was the best way of running the system.

Suffragettes were on the move, and The Society for the Prevention of Cruelty to Animals started taking a look at animal welfare. Society was beginning to think about pro-

65

viding children with some rights and protections of their own with the development of child labor laws. Things were beginning to change very gradually. Finally, in the 1960s child abuse laws were passed—and American society finally caught up with the SPCA.

Pop culture continued to expose us to a confusing set of ideas in the 1950s. It's still doing so today in the twenty-first century. Mixed-up messages about acceptable behavior were dished up in movies and in music then and now. On the one hand was (and still is) the romantic ideal. On the other hand was (and still is) a blithe acceptance of the message that violence in the family is acceptable.

Movies and TV can provide us with several examples of these types of confusing messages. Remember those old John Wayne movies where his character was as likely to give Maureen O'Sullivan a swat on the bottom as he was to give her a wet smooch on the mouth? Or how about the oldies in which the male character, after receiving a big slap across the face, takes the leading lady in his arms and smothers her with kisses. Now that last example may not sound like much. So what? You say. Hey, it was the Duke after all. He was just horsing around; all the extras in the movie thought it funny. O'Sullivan was being a brat: She deserved the spanking. Or, so what if a woman slaps a man. He's a guy, a big guy, and she's like a little fly—it's not going to hurt him.

Well maybe you know the difference, but where does it stop? Where do you draw the line between innocent fun and provocative behavior? Is physical abuse ever really justified? Doesn't it follow that if it's okay for me to use violence or to yell and scream, it must also be okay for you to do the same thing? If you follow that line of thinking, then how do you decide when enough is enough? What in the world was the message that we received from these juxta-positions of behavior supposed to be? And now, shows like *Alias* and *The Sopranos* send us the message that—what?—the family that slays together stays together? I guess so. Even some of the video games our young people buy demonstrate an appalling acceptance of violence and domination through power control.

I've asked people who have physically abused their children how they would feel if somebody twenty feet tall and 1,200 pounds took a switch to their back (or bottom, or side). I've yet to get an answer. Certainly it's all a matter of degree. Using violence, except in the case of self-defense, is simply not acceptable: It leads to only more violence.

One of the largest national violence surveys ever conducted found that in almost half of all violent episodes, women struck the first blow. Albeit, often a wimpy one by a man's standards, it was apparently in many cases enough of a provocation for the abusive situation to escalate. Men are bigger than women—most of the time. They are also responsible for seven times the serious damage to their partner. Women are catching up though. They are beginning to use weapons to retaliate.

The shelter movement of the 1970s began to draw attention to the problem of family violence, and the closed door began to open a crack. Researchers started to take a look at what was going on inside families. They came up with several ideas about how violence developed, along with its baby brother, illegitimate power and control. Several theories have been put forth, and I'll talk about seven of the most prominent ones here.

Social Leaning Theory

You remember, monkey see, monkey do? Many families who operate with dysfunctional rules are closed down families with rigid self-sustaining boundary rules. Perhaps that's what made *The Addams Family* such a silly show. They operated with outrageous rules, but they also operated in an open relationship with society—they were right out there—but in the show anyway, nobody seemed to think the family was that wacky! Everybody took the family's weirdness in stride.

In the real world, on the other hand, dysfunctional families, then and now, keep their secrets to themselves. They don't receive any reality checks from the outside that they can compare with their own behavior and problem-solving strategies. Dysfunctional families don't want these checks or strategies. They may be operating with lousy systems, but they are systems the family understands, with rules they know, and it's *their rules.* And until rather recently, if an outsider did happen to stumble upon something not quite right that was going on in somebody else's family, that outsider seemed almost embarrassed to have intruded and to have found out about it. Frequently, when the outside party colluded with the dysfunctional family, that person decided to mind his or her own business and rarely went further with any type of intervention. It still happens. Have you ever seen a parent beating on a child in a store? How did you feel about reporting it? People are afraid to get involved.

Again, the very powerful dynamics that can make family loyalty so strong can also keep an impermeable lid on family problems. As with other types of behavior, violence and power and control tactics are readily learned in one's birth family. Children who see anger tactics used in their families of origin will grow up using anger tactics or become the mate of someone who uses them. Why? Because for them it's a familiar way of settling disputes. As well, children who see violence or are treated violently are much more likely to become victims or perpetrators of violence when they become adults.

Take a minute to think about how you, as a child, learned to behave from your family. For example, how were disputes settled in your household then? How are they handled in your current relationship? Then do the following exercise. It consists of a list of behaviors that you may have witnessed as a child or things that might have happened to you.

EXERCISE
Behaviors, Then and Now

Place a check mark next to each item that applies to your experiences growing up and a check mark next to each item that applies to how you handle things now. You might end up placing two check marks next to a single item, meaning that your own behavior or the behavior of those around you hasn't changed since you were a kid.

Then | Now

1. Someone got quiet when he was angry.
2. Someone cried when she was confronted.
3. Someone left the house when he or someone else was angry.
4. Someone shouted when she was angry.
5. Someone locked someone else in a closet when he was angry.
6. Someone destroyed things when she was angry.

69

		Then	Now
7.	Someone slammed doors when he was angry.	X	X
8.	Someone cursed or insulted when she was angry.		X
9.	Someone threw things when he was angry.	X	
10.	Someone cowered when she was frightened.	X	
11.	Someone intimidated someone else when he was angry.	X	X
12.	Someone hid when she was frightened.		X
13.	Someone spit when he was angry.		
14.	Someone pulled or cut off someone else's hair when she was angry.		
15.	Someone slapped or spanked when he was angry.		X
16.	Someone bit when he was angry.		
17.	Someone burned or scalded someone else with something when she was angry.		
18.	Someone hit someone else when he was angry.	X	X
19.	Someone threw something at someone else when she was angry.	X	
20.	Someone beat someone else when he was angry.	X	
21.	Someone fondled or sexually abused someone else when he was angry.		
22.	Someone cut someone else when she was angry.		
23.	Someone shot someone when he was angry.		

70

Becoming aware that exposure to any of these anger strategies as a child may predispose you to their use in your current relationship may help you avoid the situation.

Cognitive Theory

You remember, *shoulds!* The cognitive theory regarding the development of violent traits in families goes back to the belief that children are molded by a number of things, but perhaps most important by parental messages and expectations. This theory holds that dysfunctional messages or deficits in early education regarding self-efficacy can have consequences later in life as the adult tries to respond to different situations without the appropriate tools.

Look over the following list that contains phrases describing certain characteristics associated with people who are angry or who may experience violence in their relationships. Items on this list can pertain to both males and females. See if any apply to you, because if they do, this book is for you.

An angry person or a person experiencing violence in his or her relationship may:

Have been abused as a child
Have a father who abused the mother
Have parents who were inflexible and controlling
Be jealous and possessive
Be highly controlling in relationships
Have a black-or-white view of life
Have a dual—Dr. Jekyll, Mr. Hyde—personality
Be afraid his or her spouse will leave
Use sex as aggression
Have a low opinion of women

Use denial as a coping mechanism
Use blame as a coping mechanism
Be competitive and use one-upmanship to win
Have difficulty with intimacy
Define or confirm his or her own identity through his or
  her spouse or partner
Possess a low level of self-responsibility
Be fearful of people
Have a difficult time identifying and differentiating
  feelings
Have a low tolerance for stress
Place unrealistic demands on him- or herself, spouse,
  and children
Be highly controlling in relationships
Possess a rigid coping style, not spontaneous
Have poor self-esteem
Have parents (one or both) who are alcoholic or have
  problems with drugs.

Objects Relations Theory

This is another conceptualization of how violence
develops in a relationship. Simply put, it's based on the
premise that two at-risk people find each other. Stated
another way, the objects relations theory proposes that two
people primed with some of the predisposing issues and
the same level of differentiation come together and the violence develops as a result of their synergy with each other.

Learned Helplessness

Learned helplessness is close to self-fulfilling prophecy
in some ways. It states that if you tell someone that he is a
certain thing, over time that person will become what you

tell him he is. For instance, say your child comes home from school with a grade of D on an English test, and you tell him that you're not surprised, because you never were any good at English either. Suppose you say further you bet he'll never do any better. After delivering a few more disparaging messages like that, do you imagine he's going to try harder? I don't think so. Or say you continually tell your husband he's worthless, that he's a jerk and he'll never change. Chances are you'll get what you ask for. Learned helplessness relates to anger and violence in much the same way. It suggests that after so much derogatory verbal abuse, the victim develops into the very characterization of the person who is despised. This gives the abusive person the *supposed justification* to brutalize the downtrodden partner even further. *And, this type of character assignation and cruelty is in many ways more hurtful than any physical punishment that a batterer can mete out.*

One woman I worked with in a battered women's shelter made this point beautifully. "Sara," a woman of around thirty years old, was brought into the shelter by the police after being treated for a broken arm at a local hospital. For the first few days of her stay at the shelter, Sara cried quite a bit and stayed in her room much of the time. In time, Sara began to sit in on the groups and go to counseling sessions. Gradually her sadness and isolation lessened a bit and she was ready to talk about what had happened to her. Here's her story.

She and her partner "Paul" were together for three years. In the beginning of the relationship she was flattered by all his attention. And, as is the case in many of these types of relationships, he had a great need to know of her every move. She assumed this was because he cared about her so much. She had never had so much attention in her life. Paul told her how pretty she was and complimented her on her lovely singing voice and on her skillful artwork.

Their first year together was bliss and they isolated themselves from the world. After about a year though, things started to change. During this time Sara sold some of her artwork and was beginning to make a life for herself outside of the relationship. Paul began to wonder where she was all the time and accused her of having another man on the side. He told her that her artwork was no good anymore; he said, in fact, that it stunk. He told her she was getting fat and losing her looks. He demanded that she call him hourly when she was out, and he pouted and then shouted and accused her of not loving him anymore.

One day he took away her car keys. They'd combined their bank accounts in the beginning of their relationship and now he took her name off the account. As time went by, he refused to allow her to buy clothes and cosmetics and toiletries and then told her she was filthy and smelled bad. He started calling her hurtful names. She tried to please him in the beginning, starving herself and bathing twice a day, but eventually she gave up. She felt as if she had nowhere to go, no money, and no access to a car. She stopped doing her art and sat at home becoming more and more depressed and disheveled. By the time Paul started to beat her, Sara believed what he told her about herself was true. A neighbor called the police on the night he broke her arm and knocked out her left front tooth. The police arrested Paul and took Sara to the hospital.

When Sara was finished telling her story, she said simply, "The broken bone will heal, but I don't think my heart ever will." As if on cue, like a tear, part of her front tooth dropped from her mouth. She nonchalantly picked it up from her lap, removed a tube of crazy glue from her pocket, placed a dab to the broken tooth and repositioned it in her mouth. The group remained quiet for some time. There was little anyone could say, but many of them understood perfectly.

The Disinhibition Theory

This is another theory that attempts to explain problematical relationships, and it has some plusses and minuses. In this theory, drugs and/or alcohol are blamed for anger and violence problems. Clearly there is a relationship to anger and violence in families where the use of drugs or alcohol is a problem. It has not been proven, however, that the use of either one *causes* anger or violence. They can *exacerbate* anger or violence problems due to the fact that substance abuse causes a loss of control and the loss of a person's ability to use good judgment and behave in a way that would be more appropriate in a specific situation. Drug users can have legal and family problems; they can be grooving, spaced, or just plain messed up, but there are still people who are addicts who have no problems with violence at all.

Pathology

Pathology can be to blame. Unfortunately people with personality problems are not very good candidates for change when it comes to anger or violence. Fortunately, though, this segment of the population is actually a rather small one. It is not readily treatable with traditional methods, because their anger and violence take a different shape. These people are more likely to be involved with

75

legal entities because their out-of-control behavior leaks out of the confines or their control in much more serious ways. They may require hospitalization or incarceration.

Lack of Assertion

This is the theory considered by many to be the preeminent one for understanding the roots of anger and also violence. Based within the cognitive theory framework, the lack of assertion theory hypothesizes that anger and consequently violence may be based upon a person's belief system about what is going on. It suggests that anger may stem from a person's incorrect understanding of a situation. Due to this distorted thinking pattern and due to a lack of appropriate tools to get his or her needs satisfied, the nonassertive person resorts to more primitive strategies for needs fulfillment. Subsequently, in the process, the person sabotages the chances of getting his or her needs met in a safer, more satisfying fashion.

My doctoral dissertation tested this hypothesis and agreed with other research in this regard. Subjects in my study who were better able to behave assertively and to communicate assertively were less likely to be involved in violent relationships than those who were not. *Overcoming Anger* will help you learn how to behave and communicate more assertively. But first, let's take a look at some other dynamics that you should know about that can operate in angry or violent families.

Problems Come and Go in a Cyclic Fashion

Many couples who have no violence in their relationship report a cycle similar to the type sometimes present in violent relationships. But for these couples, an angry out-burst of one sort or another takes the place of a violent one. What frequently happens when this behavioral pattern is operating is this: Things are going along quite smoothly when, for some reason, something goes out of whack.

Here's how this cyclical behavioral pattern operated in one family who came for treatment. These clients wanted to discover what they could have done differently. "Katie" and "Tony" were usually happy with their relationship and had been together for years. Sometimes, though, for reasons they didn't understand, they would have big nasty arguments.

Normally, marriage was fun for them and they enjoyed being together. Their kids were going to school, and every-body was healthy. Katie, the mom, was working part-time, volunteering, and driving carpool. Tony was doing his bit in his job as a salesman.

One day Katie decided her job really wasn't paying that much and certainly it wasn't very fulfilling so she decided to quit. She thought she'd do some research and see if she couldn't find something that not only paid more, but also offered her some advancement. She was also hoping to find a job that had a little more meaning for her or maybe even something she could do from home.

Leaving her job was a unilateral decision. Katie didn't bother to talk about it with Tony, which was unusual. This couple had a good relationship and were usually on the same sheet of music when it came to making decisions. Usually they discussed decisions like this. But heck, Katie thought this is no big deal. This job was paying her virtu-ally zero. It was not enough to change their style of living or the quality of their lives. So, she went ahead and made the decision on her own.

Upon hearing about her decision, Tony was stunned. Tony had his own agenda. Things hadn't been going so well at work, because Tony was a salesman who relied pretty heavily on his commissions, and business had been slow for the last couple of months. He hadn't mentioned this to Katie. He was trying to be a good guy and not worry her. Never mind that he hadn't communicated with *her*, here he was, trying to do the right thing and she hadn't consulted him first. He felt hurt, but instead of sharing what he was feeling, he "harrumphed" and walked out of the room. Katie felt unsupported.

The next week Tony distanced himself. Since she wasn't working, Katie had more time for the household, so she cleaned like a maniac and cooked big dinners. But Tony pouted and worked late. He missed the dinners and didn't notice how great the house looked. In fact he criticized her housekeeping. Katie thought he was being thoughtless and selfish. He continued to come home late.

By the end of the week Katie found a job opportunity she thought would be exciting. She called Tony at work to tell him about it. He was tied up in meetings all day and didn't return her call. Katie was hurt and angry, so she called a babysitter and went out for a dinner with friends. Meanwhile, Tony had had a good day and decided to surprise Katie by taking her out for dinner. When he pulled up to the house, he saw the babysitter's car in the driveway. He asked the sitter where Katie had gone, and she told him Katie was having dinner with her girlfriends. Making the assumption that Katie had planned yet another thing behind his back, Tony stewed until Katie returned. As soon as the babysitter left, he blew up. No big surprise there!

The couple came in to the office to discuss what had

happened. During the session Katie and Tony were asked to go back and, as couple, try to determine what their unexpressed feelings had actually been each step of the way. When explored in retrospect, the progression of blunders they both had made were easy to identify. Unexpressed feelings of confusion, hurt, sadness, and annoyance all took on different aspects in each of their personal attempts to armor themselves against their more vulnerable feelings.

In a "tit for tat" fashion Katie and Tony had upped the ante. Each had backed the other into having to play for higher stakes. In their particular situation, the couple agreed they could have diffused what became a more and more tense situation that eventually terminated in a blowup. They marveled at how one innocuous event led to another and how each event had taken on a life of its own. This was a strong couple, remember. If Tony had shared his feeling of worry with Katie, or if Katie had checked in with Tony at the beginning, a rotten week might have been avoided.

Finally the couple explored whether any of their behaviors pushed buttons at deeper levels as their week of miscommunication and frustration unraveled itself. Katie remembered that when she was little, her father used to behave in much the same way Tony had over the preceding week. Her father's usual tactic was to distance himself from the family and stay away from home for extended periods of time. Tony remembered that his mother would shut down and give his dad the silent treatment.

Old messages and poor communication had pushed this otherwise happy couple to behave in a way that they never intended to. One thing escalated into another until a point of crisis and catharsis occurred. Because the relationship was a good one, the crisis point was relatively low. Because the family was open, the incident acted as a catalyst for them to seek help in straightening out what was going on. Unfortunately, in more troubled families, it frequently takes more upheaval and more pain before the couple gets some help.

Over the course of the next couple of sessions, Katie and Tony worked on finding strategies to nip problems in the bud and avoid hurtful and angry blowups. This book will provide you with several of the strategies they learned.

People May Wear a Few Different Hats

Many relationships involve a dynamic where each partner assumes one role for a time and then flips into another and then another. You can envision the different roles as a triangle. On the left side of the triangle you find the role of persecutor. On the right side you find the role of victim. On the bottom part of this triangle you find the role of the rescuer. This pattern of behavior can be found in angry families and in violent ones. Depending on the situation and depending on how well people are getting their needs met, they assume one role or another. The roles flip-flop like this:

1. The persecutor uses angry or threatening behavior to get what he wants.
2. Although there may be a lot of satisfaction over "winning," there may also be some residual guilt, so the persecutor turns into the rescuer. (Perhaps that's why after an argument, many people report great love making. Or maybe that's the reason the victim is

typically rewarded with flowers or some other form of indulgence after the outburst.)

3. Then, the former victim, feeling vindicated, and for the present time more powerful, may assume the role of persecutor in order to get even. You can see how this pattern of behavior could self-perpetuate in a dysfunctional relationship.

Here's how this type of role reversal operated in "Teri" and "Jack's" relationship.

Jack had come for counseling in order to help him get through his divorce from Teri. He was going through the grieving process and trying to determine how things had wound up as they had.

Teri and Jack had met while on a ski trip three years before. Jack and a couple of his buddies decided to take a lesson, and Teri was their instructor. She was athletic and pretty and Jack was immediately infatuated. They went out several times that week and then Jack went back home. They corresponded and Teri came to visit. Everything was very romantic. Teri went back and forth from California to Colorado, and their fairy-tale courtship continued to intensify. Sometimes, though, Jack would call and she wouldn't call back for days or weeks at time. Other times Teri would call in tears and accuse him of not loving her. He really didn't know what to make of her unusual behavior, but he was in love and didn't worry about it too much.

After a few months, with very little time together under their belts, they decided to get married. Teri quit her job and moved to California. A couple of months into the marriage, odd things started happening. Since Jack was a police officer, his duty schedule changed with some frequency. One time he came home to find the apartment torn apart. He explored the apartment's four rooms and discovered Teri sitting on a disheveled bed with a bunch of torn-up photographs scattered around her. Jack was at first concerned, thinking some intruder had caused the confusion. No, explained Teri, that wasn't what happened. She was mad because she found some pictures of Jack and another girl, so she wrecked the apartment. Jack was, understandably, very annoyed and yelled at Teri that she was acting crazy. He used a few other expletives to drive his thoughts home.

Teri broke down. She threw herself on the bed and cried her heart out. She told Jack she didn't know what had gotten into her and that she was very, very sorry. She appeared to be so contrite that Jack felt like a louse, making her cry so much. He kissed her and he cuddled her and he gently put her to bed and then cleaned up the mess in the rest of the apartment.

On another occasion, Jack pulled night duty for several evenings in a row. Teri didn't like being left alone so she decided to try to get Jack home. She called the officer on duty and told him that she just found out that Jack was having an affair and that she needed him to come home in order to discuss the situation. The officer asked Jack what was going on. Jack told his superior officer he was clueless and didn't know what Teri was talking about. Nonetheless, Jack was told to go home.

Embarrassed and mortified, he once again blew up at Teri. On this occasion, Teri didn't back down; she came right back at him using "the best defense is a good offense" strategy. Then Teri abruptly stopped screaming, approached Jack, and gave him a hug and a kiss. She told him everything was okay and that she wasn't mad at him for yelling at her. They had a great time in bed and Jack felt mollified, if a bit confused.

The marriage finally came to an end when Jack returned home from work one afternoon to find Teri and another man in bed together. Jack had once again been cast as the victim. At this point in the situation, Teri was entrenched in her role as the persecutor. Jack went ballistic when he saw them together and ordered the guy to get out of the house. He continued to argue with Teri, cursing at her and at the same time telling her how much she had hurt him. In other words, Jack assumed the role of the persecutor.

When Jack took on his new role, Teri flipped out of her role as she fell to the floor crying. Just like clockwork and true to form, she assumed the role of the victim. Jack was now feeling he was in the power position and subsequently he felt like he could be magnanimous. He decided he could afford to be gracious and rescue poor Teri, so he went over to her and embraced her, at which point she bit him on the pectoral muscle, hard. That was the final straw. Jack woke up and walked out.

Now he sat in my office trying to understand the dynamics that had sucked him into an unhealthy relationship in which he continually felt bad about himself. He had fallen victim to powerful gamesmanship. But, fortunately for Jack, he left the game before it was too late.

Take Me to Your Leader

Another pattern that may develop in families subjected to the tyranny of violence or anger and the threat of violence

83

is one that resembles the phenomenon known as the Stockholm syndrome. The Stockholm syndrome is the name given to a constellation of behaviors that frequently develop among people who are held hostage. It can develop as the result of the use of tactics not unlike those used on prisoners of war. The Stockholm syndrome also provides us with an explanation of why abused children will defend their abusive parent and beg to stay with them even when they are at risk of further abuse or injury.

These behaviors develop due to techniques used by the captor or, in family relationships, by the person with the power and control. The bottom line is, people tend to want to join with the people who have the power. You could say that these techniques are the extreme form of Machiavellian disinterest and are extremely powerful tools for gaining compliance. It will be helpful for you to become aware of the techniques used by controlling individuals and discover if any of them are operating in your relationships.

Degradation

This type of treatment can take the form of low-level verbal assaults and put-downs that are damaging to a person's self-esteem. At the upper end of the spectrum, degradation may involve actually confining someone to a locked room and forcing that person to remain filthy or nude. This type of treatment reduces the victim to very basic concerns like being allowed to go to the bathroom or take a bath or get a blanket.

Enforcement of Trivial Demands

In this situation, the person in control sees to it that demeaning and meaningless demands are met. This type of demand might be something as unnecessary as asking somebody to rearrange the dishwasher in a certain way or refold all the towels differently. Due to the random nature of these demands, the underdog becomes confused, wary, and vigilant, wondering what will come next. Every move the underdog makes becomes potentially dangerous for him. This tactic develops the habit of compliance.

Granting Occasional Indulgences

This type of intermittent positive reinforcement provides motivation for continued compliance. This on-again-off-again reinforcement agenda is the most powerful, because it allows for the captive to remain hopeful of a positive outcome as long as he or she cooperates.

Inducing Debility and Exhaustion

Treatment like this might manifest itself as continually waking one's partner from sleep or interrupting the partner when he or she is in the middle of some task. It's crazy making and it weakens a person's mental and physical ability to resist.

Demonstrations of Omnipotence

These maneuvers serve quite simply to suggest the futility of resistance. The person with the power finds a means that shows the weaker one that she'll never win.

You can bet in the movie *The Godfather*, when Johnny Fontaine awoke to find his horse's head at the foot of his bed, he got the message loud and clear that Don Corleone was pretty darned omnipotent and he'd better pay attention to him.

Threatening Behavior

At its most basic, threatening behavior cultivates an atmosphere of anxiety and despair. There's an old story that may explain what this type of behavior might look like. It goes something like this:

In the old West there once lived a rancher who decided it was high time to find himself a wife. Since there was no likely candidate in the surrounding area, the rancher, a no-nonsense kind of fella, decided a mail-order bride would do just fine. The rancher was not one to waste time so he went down to the Western Union office in town where he sent a telegram to a mail-order outfit he'd heard about in Kansas City. The telegram enumerated his needs and the necessary qualifications for his bride-to-be.

In due course, a likely lady was found. A contract was drawn up and all the arrangements were made all proper. A fortnight later, when the rancher's lady arrived at the train station, the rancher greeted her pleasantly. Being a no-nonsense kind of fella and not one to waste time, the rancher then escorted this lady over to the town's courthouse, where a justice of the peace hitched the two of them. It was a fine little ceremony.

One of the town ladies, Mrs. Maudy, saw the two of them exit the courthouse and sashayed over to see what was up. She sidled up to the new bride and inquired just as nice as you please, who might this lady be and what might she be doing in town. The rancher turned toward Mrs. Maudy and in a not-so-nice fashion told her, "Mrs. Maudy, that is none of your business!" His new bride was somewhat shocked, but she said nothing.

They started back toward the buckboard that was to convey them to the ranch. The rancher confided to his wife,

"That durned Mrs. Maudy, she's a terrible gossip. I don't need the whole town knowin' my business." He shook his head in disgust and smiled at his bride. "I never could abide it." The rancher helped his bride and her luggage on to the cart and told the chestnut mare "gaddap." The horse was slow to respond so the rancher cracked his whip in the air over the animal's head and yelled at the nag, "Gaddap you lazy thing!" The horse complied. "Laziness," the rancher said and shook his head in disgust. He smiled at his wife. "I never could abide it."

About a half mile from town the newlyweds came upon a gang of boys shooting marbles in the road. The rancher told the kids to get out of the way and cracked his whip in the air. One of the kids told the rancher to go around them as there was plenty of room. The rancher took out his Colt and shot it in the air. "Get out of my way you durned rascals!" They got out of the way. His new bride was somewhat shocked, but she said nothing. The rancher replaced his gun in its holster. "Smart-aleck kids," he said. He shook his head in disgust and smiled at his bride. "I never could abide 'em."

The rancher and his wife went on. The ranch house was finally in sight. As they approached, an old donkey ambled onto the road, blocking the way. "Get out of my way," the rancher called. He got no response from the spavined thing. Next he took out his whip and cracked it over the beast's head—still nothing. Finally, the rancher took out his Colt and shot it in the air. The donkey swished his tail. The rancher pointed his gun and shot the unfortunate donkey dead. His new bride was somewhat shocked, but she said nothing. Once again the rancher holstered his weapon. "Stubbornness," he said. He shook his head in disgust and smiled at his wife. "I never could abide it."

He helped her down from the cart and headed toward the tidy ranch house. As they got close, the bride noticed a headstone off to the right. She approached it and her husband followed her. "That's the grave of my first wife, Martha," the rancher said. "Oh that woman had a mind of her own, she did." He shook his head in disgust and smiled at his wife. "I never could abide it." He walked toward the ranch house stoop. His new bride turned and took a look back at the road. She followed her husband into her new home.

Monopolizing One's Perception

This technique eliminates any type of stimuli that may compete with the personal agenda of the person in power. It fixes the weaker person's attention on his or her immediate predicament and it fosters introspection into the situation. The person becomes more and more distanced from the world and its reality checks and instead becomes fixated on the present. This technique frustrates all actions that are not consistent with the power person's rules for compliance. The person whose perception is monopolized becomes more and more concerned with the details of following the rules to the letter, to the exclusion of caring for him- or herself or caring about the situation.

Isolation

In this situation victims are deprived of all social support systems that might supply them with an ability to resist the whims of the one in control. The people trapped develop an intense concern for themselves and their relationship with their controllers. In hostage situations, isolation helps in making captives dependent upon their captors for news of the outside world and all of their basic needs. Isolation can be translated into a relationship when one partner forbids the other to associate with friends or with family, and the stronger partner controls all incoming information.

Five Power Trips

There's nothing wrong with having power or with using power if it's done legitimately. There are a few types of power you may want to review in order to decide if you are using power or abusing it. Each type has its uses, some good, some not so good.

1. **Legitimate power.** This is the kind of power that is derived from position and includes power coming from elected or selected positions. An example of legitimate power would include things like presidential power, the power a minister has to marry someone, or a captain's power to command his sailors and run his ship.

2. **Referent power.** This type of power refers to that which is derived from one's personal characteristics. Examples of this kind of power could include traits like affability, amiability, likeability, and personal charisma.

3. **Expert power.** In this category, power comes from somebody's greater expertise or knowledge in a specific area. Examples of this type of power include that of a teacher in the classroom or a doctor doing surgery. You wouldn't want the woman from the dry cleaner's working on your appendix.

4. **Reward power.** This power is derived from the ability to give benefits to another person, ranging from monetary to psychological benefits. Used benignly there is no problem with it. Examples of appropriate use of this type of power include congratulating someone on a job well done or giving a good worker a raise. Problems arise when reward is used in a way that keeps someone in line as a means of controlling that person.

5. **Coercive power.** This type of power is derived from the ability to punish. Examples of this type of power include the power a judge uses to sentence a felon or the power a priest uses to excommunicate someone. Although reward power is a potentially tricky one, coercive power is really the one with the most problems on a personal level. Coercive power is the power used to control another in a relationship This punitive means of control is the one you need to watch out for and determine if it's operating your relationship.

Are You in Control or Out of Control?

If you're concerned because you identified with the kinds of controlling techniques you've read about in this chapter, you may want to look for any areas of your life where you feel you are either trying to control or being controlled. Areas of control to watch out for are:

- **Financial.** Do you try to control your partner's finances? Is your partner trying to control yours? Obviously, when there's been an agreement about money matters, there's no need for concern. If your husband is a spendthrift and the two of you decided he operates better when he's on an allowance, that's fine. There would be a concern, though, if a husband or wife took total control for no good reason or where money was doled out, or not doled out, as a reward or a punishment for specific behavior. Has you spouse ever tried to keep you from getting a job when you wanted some of your own personal income? Have you ever tried that with your partner? Other ways this power might be demonstrated are when one partner forces another to beg for money or takes away a checkbook or credit card.

- **Emotional.** Do you try to control your spouse by granting, or not granting, sexual or emotional favors? Do you play mind games with your spouse or worry about your spouse's mood? When you're mad, do you ever try to make your spouse feel guilty? Do you humiliate your partner? Do you resort to using put-downs when you're angry? Does your partner make you feel guilty or humiliate you? Do you or your mate use the silent treatment to get what you want? Do you ever try to make your partner feel as if he or she is crazy?

- **Use the children.** Do you or your partner use the children in order to relay messages to each other? Do either you or your spouse or ex-spouse use the kids to make each other feel guilty? Do either one of you threaten to take the children away when you're angry? If you're separated, do either of you use visitation issues to harass each other?

- **Minimization and denial.** Do you or your partner make light of serious issues or behave in a condescending way toward each other? Do you shift responsibility, and blame your partner for mistakes you made? Do you tell your partner that it is his or her fault that you had a fight? When angry, does your partner try this maneuver on you?

- **Coercion or threatening behavior.** Have you ever made a threat, or carried one out, against your mate? Has your spouse ever threatened to leave you or commit suicide in order to get his or her way about some issue? Has your mate ever tried to get you to do something illegal or report you for something? Have you ever done something like this to your mate?

- **Intimidation.** Do you or your spouse try to make one or the other afraid with your looks, gestures, or the things that you do? Does your spouse smash or destroy your property? Do you ever break your mate's belongings? Has a family pet ever been abused?

If you find that you recognize any of these dynamics, you're not alone. They happen to a greater or lesser degree in many, many families. There are, however, much better ways of getting your needs met and having a happy, successful relationship. The following chapters provide you some new ideas and strategies for improving the way you feel about your relationships.

5

Stress
and Emotions

Let's face it, most of us hate change—even good change can be downright stressful. Nonetheless, change and the stress that results are facts of life. It's worth taking a look at the role stress plays in your life. By examining how stressful change affects you, you can learn better ways of handling the emotions stress causes, and that includes handling anger. Stress and anger are kissing cousins—your stress level directly contributes to your anger level. This chapter helps you identify some of the many different types of stress that may be affecting you and the techniques to control that stress.

Do you feel that stress is taking over your life and making you feel overwhelmed? Just remember that the cognitive management of anger and stress is predicated upon your having some power and some choices about how they affect you and your life. The following exercise will help you define stress and how it may be affecting your life.

Once you have a better understanding of what stresses you out and how stress operates on your behavior, you can take the first steps toward responding in less unhealthy and negative ways.

EXERCISE
How Stress Affects Me

1. What is your definition of stress?

_____

_____

2. Rate your current level of stress:

   a. Low
   b. Medium
   c. High
   d. Off the charts

3. Are there things going on in your life that are very stressful for you? List some of them.

_____

_____

4. What do you do to manage your stress?

_____

_____

5. How do you respond to stress?

_____

_____

Positive and Negative Stress

Stress will be around as long as you are, and like anger, it's not necessarily a bad thing. Stress is just a nonspecific response to any demand that your environment places upon you. Every time you give your kids a bath, get your haircut, or sit stopped in traffic, you have to adjust to changing situational demands. Stress keeps us aware and functioning. Like an alarm clock or a crying baby, it wakes us up and gets us moving. Without it we'd veg out all day. Without stress, our systems become inactive. Inactive systems are unproductive and inherently fall apart over time. If nothing much is happening to keep them tuned up and running, things tend to fall apart like old cars in a junk yard.

If stress stays at an optimal level, individuals function very well. We each have a personal "perfect" stress level. When we operate within the limits of that stress level, we perform at peak levels. For example, if you have a career that provides you with interesting challenges or achievements, you are likely to be performing at a peak level. On the other hand, if your work situation constantly overwhelms you or your job bores you to tears, your performance is likely to be spotty at best and disastrous at worst. Becoming aware of how much positive stress motivates you is important. Stress keeps us peppy. As we continually adjust to environmental influences, we are forced to adapt or accommodate new information and challenges. In this regard stress can always be seen as positive; it keeps things interesting and stimulating.

Stress can be positive stress or negative stress. Positive stress is the result of a situation that, in the normal scheme of things, is considered to be a "happy" event. Pregnancy, Christmas, vacations, and the like are occasions of positive stress. But sometimes even these occasions don't seem very positive. For instance, you may be reminded of horrible pregnancies complete with raging hormones and endless morning sickness. Or Christmas, normally considered a time of happiness for many, might evoke for you those awful Christmases at Aunt Bertha's where Uncle George invariably got smashed and passed out in his green-bean-and-French-fried-onion casserole.

The point is, even things that make you happy by changing your life in positive ways can also be stressful in a negative way. Left to run amuck, even *good things* have the potential to put you at risk for anger due to the stress on your system. True, there are two sides to the stress coin, but once again, awareness is key. Remember, you have a choice about how you handle stress.

Work on the following exercise to assess how much stress you are experiencing in your life. Then we'll talk later in this chapter about how to handle the various events that have caused your stress.

EXERCISE
On Again–Off Again Stressors

Look over this list of intermittent stressful situations. Each one is rated according to the level of stress it produces, 10 being the highest. Add up the total point values of all the events that occurred in your life in the past twelve months.

Intermittent Stressor	Points
1. My spouse died.	10
2. My relationship ended.	10
3. A close friend or family member died.	9
4. I or my spouse went to jail.	9
5. I suffered a serious injury or illness.	8

Intermittent Stressor	Points
6. I got married.	8
7. I experienced sexual difficulties.	7
8. I or my partner got pregnant.	7
9. I reconciled with my spouse.	7
10. I got fired.	7
11. I changed jobs.	6
12. I had a child leave home.	5
13. I moved.	5
14. My income greatly increased.	4
15. I began or ended going to school.	4
16. I took out a large loan or mortgage.	4
17. I had trouble with friends or neighbors.	4
18. My income greatly decreased.	4
19. My spouse started or stopped working.	3
20. I changed my eating/drinking habits.	3
21. I stopped smoking.	3
22. I had trouble with my boss.	3
23. I gained a new family member.	3
24. I had legal problems.	3
25. I had a significant car accident.	3
26. I was promoted.	3

Total your score to determine your current stress level. If you scored over 100, you'll benefit from learning some of the management techniques you'll find in the next chapter.

Next, do the following exercise to see if you have ongoing stressors and rate how much they affect you.

EXERCISE
My Ongoing Stressors

Place a check next to any event that occurred in your life in the past twelve months. Some of these items may be positive and others negative, but they all are stress provoking and potentially angering. Rate each item that is true for you on a scale from 1 to 10, with 10 having the most impact.

Ongoing Stressor		Points
1. I commute long distances in heavy traffic.	○	_____
2. My neighborhood is not safe.	○	_____
3. I lack adequate privacy.	○	_____
4. I don't have a good support system.	○	_____
5. I have a chronically ill mate or child.	○	_____
6. I have continuing relationship conflicts.	○	_____
7. I have a family member with severe problems.	○	_____
8. I'm not able to express my feelings.	○	_____
9. I lack sufficient income.	○	_____

Ongoing Stressor		Points
10. I have problems with drugs or alcohol.	○	____
11. I live in an abusive household.	○	____
12. My spouse has problems with drugs or alcohol.	○	____
13. My job security is shaky.	○	____
14. My work is boring or I'm overqualified.	○	____
15. I have no control over things that affect me.	○	____
16. I am not in good health.	○	____
17. I travel for work much of the time.	○	____
18. I have a great job with a lot of responsibility.	○	____
19. My workload or schedule creates problems.	○	____
20. I'm concerned about the political and economic situation in this country.	○	____

If you scored over 100, you're at high risk for stress-related problems and you'll benefit from the techniques covered in this chapter and in Chapter 7.

External and Internal Stress

Stress can come at you in two ways: externally and internally. I'll talk about external stress first. External stress can be provoked by external *impersonal* stressors and external *personal* stressors. The exercise you just completed contains examples of both.

External impersonal stressors are, generally speaking, things that are served up to you, or thrown on your plate, as it were. These are things over which you have no control because they are random acts of the universe. Examples include the attack on the World Trade Center, floods, gas shortages, hurricanes, and wars. In most cases you have no choice over whether or not you experience external impersonal stressors; with the proper stress management tools, you will be able to acknowledge two very important things:

1. You are not responsible for creating the specific situation.
2. You have very little control over the situation.

So far so good—that is, if you can always recognize these externally caused situational stressors as random acts of the universe outside of you're control. But based on where you're coming from and even what kind of day you're having, external impersonal stressors can develop their own gestalt and a meaning far greater than the sum of their parts. So, even if you experience a bunch of little stuff that starts gnawing at you, after a while these occurrences can eventually build into an extremely angering situation. As a result, you may begin to take personally those situations over which you have no control, translating an external impersonal stressor into an external personal stressor. This can lead to trouble because then you're just one step away from turning them into internal stressors that operate on your belief system.

Internal stressors eat away at your sense of mastery and self-esteem and are difficult to deal with. There was a TV commercial awhile back that made this point beautifully. The scene opened on a nattily attired young guy waiting to cross a street in a busy city. The camera showed his full body at first, but then went in for a close-up of his face. In the meantime, background music like the kind in *Jaws* began to build. The strident notes added to the comic and dramatic effect of the guy's rather horrified facial expression as he looked up to the sky. There, above, circled some type of bird of prey, a raven or hawk, a bird of omen. The shot focused in on the man's face again and then quickly cut back to what he was looking at; it was his car! The camera flashed back to the sinister bird. Finally, the man began to run, hell-bent-for-leather, across the street, disregarding all the traffic, flinging himself protectively on the hood of his vehicle. His paint job was saved from the evil intent of the circling bird. Hurrah!

Silly? Yes, but effective nonetheless. Why? Because we can all relate to just this type of thinking. But the logic of this scenario and the young man's reckless behavior does not make sense in the "real world." This commercial effectively demonstrates how easily we can turn an external impersonal stressor into an external personal stressor. This is exactly the kind of behavior that we should avoid.

Sometimes it just seems as if, from the minute you wake up until the minute you nod off at night, nothing in the day was meant to go smoothly. But it's important not to let your perception turn into an external personal stressor, because negative belief systems can be very strong, not to mention very seductive. After a couple of lousy days in a row, it's no wonder you begin to feel an angering sense of futility and lack of mastery. But take heed: *Your ability to identify the stress you are dealing with and determining its source can become powerful allies in managing your emotions.*

Take a minute to go back over the list of stressors in the last exercise. Try to identify external impersonal stressors and differentiate them from the more personal stressors. Which ones do you have more of in your life? External stressors are generally managed with stress management techniques, such as exercise and meditation, which we'll get to a bit later in Chapter 8. Unfortunately, external stress that is not dealt with can lead to internal stress and turmoil. Fortunately, internal stress is within your domain to do something about; over this internal kingdom you have total power and control. It's all about your belief system! And you can learn to manage that! In Chapters 7, 8, 9, and 10 you'll learn how.

Anger, Schmanger—Context Is Key

In terms of what makes you angry and what stresses you out, it is crucial to examine how you interpret what is happening to you. You have to look at the context in which the event occurs in order to discover if the stressor is indeed something that is truly a threat. Context is key!

Imagine that your workday is over and your spouse has called you just as you're leaving your job and asked you to stop at the market for a carton of milk. You're beat, but you're willing. You're just about to park when you notice a transient is panhandling by the door you had intended to use. Since you would rather avoid this potentially irksome person, you take a little calming breath and go around to the side entrance.

Once in the store, you locate the milk and find the

express line. A tiny, fragile old lady comes up and asks if she can go ahead of you. She has a little can of cat food and tells you she's not feeling well and would like to get home as soon as she can. Hoping the cat food really is her cat's dinner and not hers, you tell the lady, well sure, and feel maybe only slightly put off.

Here's another scenario. This time instead of the lady, it's two burly tank-topped and tattooed types who shove past you as if you're not there. Not so clean smelling, they plunk down a few bottles of Colt, some bean dip, and tortilla chips. One of them says, hey man, you don't mind do you? It's likely that this pair is going to bug you more than the little old lady.

The little old lady may annoy you or you may sympathize with her. You may let her go ahead of you simply because you don't want her to pass out in back of you. You may see the existential finality of life in her or you may just like cats. Whatever the reason, she is unlikely to be someone whom you find to be stress or anger provoking. And what the heck, in reality you probably do have a little more time than she does—in the cosmic sense. On the other hand, those two guys, well, several adjectives come to mind—obnoxious, rude, crude, dangerous if crossed, scary. Certainly the approach of the two guys is more anger evoking than that of the little old lady. Maybe you feel pushed around by the men or that they have taken advantage of you.

Hopefully, this example demonstrates how two situations, which have a similar impact (you probably will get home with the milk at about the same time either way), might trigger two very different belief systems. It's all in the context. Your reaction will be due to your beliefs about the two situations and the impact they have on you.

Adaptation and Accommodation— The Way I See It

Every time you encounter a stressor, you are forced to cope with it in one of two ways: adaptation or accommodation.

Adaptation is an outside coping strategy that requires you to *change yourself* in some way. For instance, the temperature in the theater changes and the lights go dim. You put on a sweater to warm up and use your glasses to see a little better. It's kind of like saying, "Okay, I can go along with this. I guess I have to if I want to be comfortable."

Accommodation, on the other hand, is an inside coping strategy that you can use to combat stress. It requires that you incorporate the new stressor into an underlying conceptual framework that you already have in place. For example, say you're a fanatic alpine skier, and your belief system tells you, "Alpine skiing is the best winter sport." One weekend your friends insist you try snowboarding. You do. After three days of mortification, you get pretty good and discover you really enjoy it. *Because of your new experience, you're forced to add a new concept to your old conceptual framework and adjust your belief system to: "Alpine skiing and snowboarding are the best winter sports."* You haven't really chucked the old idea; you just tuned it up a bit. Voilà, you have successfully accommodated a stressor!

All Those Gadgets and Information Overload

On top of the daily stressors we must endure, the boom of the Information Age may have actually increased our stress levels. It's called "information overload." Although we may love (and in some cases almost worship) our labor-saving gismos, at some level they may be causing us more stress than they're worth. Have you ever felt like bashing your computer screen in frustration when you can't get those annoying pop-ups to go away? Have you ever felt like throwing your telephone at the wall after wasting time listening to endless electronic options and never getting a human on the line?

It makes sense for us to look around at our environments and decide what we really want in our lives. We can make active choices to moderate the effects of all the tools we now take for granted and utilize to keep up with the Joneses, stay knowledgeable, stay current, and one step ahead of our competitors—all of the things that cause unnecessary stress.

The relatively recent marvels of fax machines, PCs, answering machines, cell phones, and pagers serve as surrogate servants, secretaries, and answering services. They are essential in many instances, but their contributions can be a double-edged sword. In keeping us in touch, tuned-in, and on call, they don't allow us the opportunity for any downtime. The notion of being "unavailable" has become taboo. One fed-up client has tried to take a stand, sort of. His e-mail address is *leavesamalone@hotmail.com*.

Not too many years ago, society had some downtime built in. On weekends, most people got together with friends and family and relaxed or went to ball games and picnics. On Sundays, they read the funnies and went to church. Maybe they had a barbeque.

Now, with today's frenetic pace, you may *have* to go shopping or to the market or to the drugstore just to get a head start on the week. You may need to use your weekend time to get online to tackle that unfinished work project. At just the touch of a button, you can be connected to work all day and night. But is all this activity really what you need to stay calm, healthy, and balanced?

The list of "convenient" technology is boggling. ATMs may have made banking easier, but now you risk being mugged anytime day or night. Cell phones are a great convenience, but there is concern they can cause traffic accidents and maybe cancer. Every day, through various means of media, we are bombarded with advertising urging us to indulge in the latest trends in fashion, health, and medicine. Heaven forbid we should fall behind in our quest to be trendy.

Even the evening news subjects us to stress. We learn daily from our hometown news anchors all about natural disasters, killings, and babies dumped in dumpsters, not to mention constant reminders about terrorism and threats of war.

Today's kids don't escape this deluge of stress, either. Children are primed early for pressure. For some little ones, expectations regarding sports, grades, and popularity start during the preschool years. The pressure continues through high school, where advanced placement classes have become almost mandatory for college admission.

Sure, people probably were concerned about the advance of technology and the quickening pace of life when the telegraph was developed and the telephone came along and loused up the fine art of letter writing, but today's technology is proliferating at a truly remarkable pace. Improved telecommunications has made many of us totally accessible at all times. Is it healthy for us to be so available? Take inventory of the unnecessary stressors in your life. What can you do to lessen the load and recharge your battery?

Back to the Garden

While you certainly can't escape or ignore technology, there are ways that you can take charge of the amount of stress you allow your environment to dish out to you. Perhaps you could avoid watching the news or forgo watching TV altogether and read a book instead. Maybe you could job share or work a four-day week. Maybe you'd like to devote some special time to yourself. Perhaps you can think of a hobby you'd like to pursue. Could you ride a bike to work?

Take a minute to think about your situation. Write down one thing that you would like to change in order to get a better handle on your stress. It is absolutely appropriate to allow yourself some choices in determining what stressful situations are necessary. It is also absolutely appropriate to decide what level of stress is comfortable or acceptable in your life and what stressors you can afford to do without. Identification is the first step to stress and anger management. Taking responsibility is the second.

Remember, in managing internal stressors, you are the boss. Take a minute to do the next exercise to find out how responsible you are for your personal thoughts and actions.

EXERCISE
How Responsible Am I
for My Thoughts and Actions?

Indicate by filling in a percent how responsible you feel for the following aspects of your life. Think about whether your feelings of responsibility are appropriate or within your control. Do you find yourself becoming angry, confused, frightened, resentful, or frustrated when you think about examples of these situations?

Thought or Action	**Percent**

1. Problems that arise in the family   _____ %

   Example:_____

2. Mistakes that involve you   _____ %

   Example:_____

3. Acting on your decisions   _____ %

   Example:_____

4. Staying optimistic about situations   _____ %

   Example:_____

5. Finding things to be happy about   _____ %

   Example:_____

6. Finding constructive solutions to personal problems _____ %

   Example:_____

7. Working out win/win solutions to interpersonal
   problems   _____ %

   Example:_____

8. Things that happen to you   _____ %

   Example:_____

9. Finding positive people to be with   _____ %

   Example:_____

10. Taking care of yourself and your health   _____ %

   Example:_____

Thought or Action	Percent
11. Taking care of business	_____ %
Example:_____	
12. Taking care of others	_____ %
Example:_____	
13. Managing your time	_____ %
Example:_____	
14. Making other people happy	_____ %
Example:_____	

If completing this exercise helped you remember any situations that evoked any negative emotions, now's the time to start managing your internal stress. In looking over your answers, you may have found areas in your life for which you feel you bear appropriate responsibility. In other areas, you may have discovered that you need to assume a bit more. In still other areas, you may have realized that you have been trying to be responsible for things that are not your problem. Examine your role in them and decide if your position of responsibility needs an overhaul.

Now, take a piece of paper and write down any additional situational stressors, either external or internal, that have come up for you recently. Decide if the situation was within your control. Then ask yourself what you could have done in each case to improve the way in which you reacted.

6

Burnout

As the Broadway musical *Annie* (and now even Mini Me in the Austin Powers movies) reminds us, "It's a hard-knock life!" In order to get along and in order to provide for our needs, most of us have to work—and that can put us at great risk for anger due to burnout.

The second half of the last century and the beginning of this one have born witness to tremendous change both in terms of technology and in terms of society itself. Since World War II, America in particular has experienced revolutionary change in the way people work and in the way they think. American society, once very personal, has become almost anonymous. Doors stay closed and shutters stay drawn. Everyone minds his or her own business for the most part. Everybody is so busy just trying to get the job done and to accomplish what needs to be accomplished that little time is left for us to replenish ourselves and get our needs met. It's no wonder people get angry and frustrated. It can be tough out there!

Within one generation almost all the rules went out the door. Rules governing behavior and morality that were once well established morphed or disappeared altogether, and expectations regarding performance and competence skyrocketed. People who grew up believing in the Ten Commandments are now faced with rock and gangsta rap filled with violence and disrespect. People who once believed in the notion that if you work hard, you will achieve your goals, have come face to face with athletes and entertainers who rake in the megabucks for what appears to be less than the usual effort. People who grew up outside on playgrounds now have kids growing up inside with play stations. All this change and seemingly contradictory values, plus all those good old parental *shoulds*, create quite a setup for falling victim to very angering, crazy-making double-binds. So it's not a surprise that burnout can take its toll on you and make you considerably more anger prone.

Welcome to the New Millennium

It's an information technology world! Just to maintain our footing in the workplace these days, we need to continually learn new techniques and excel in what we do. Information and technology have become a religion of sorts for many people. Better keep your computer updated, otherwise it might not be able to read the new software that's constantly being generated. You'd better get yourself out there and buy a couple new TVs, too, because by 2006, analogue signals are set to go digital. Pressure from the outside world bombards us with higher and higher expectations.

In order to apply structure to our lives and avoid information overload, we are forced to become selective. We learn how to compartmentalize—we have to. Who wants to spend time and energy worrying about all the awful stuff that could happen? We are forced to screen out the excessive information and stimulation, and erect barriers to protect ourselves. The awful stuff gets buried, sure, but at some level it's still there and it's still working on us. This denial and maintenance program is a difficult one and can create more stress and anger. In order to maintain these barriers, we expend a lot of negative energy and may also squelch our ability to maintain close relationships, find ways in which we can rejuvenate ourselves, and explore how we are feeling.

Although we may have achieved affluence and prestige, we might have given up the people part of the equation. We may have lost the feelings of connectedness that we need in order to feel good about ourselves. Eventually, we may bow under the weight of this frustration, and then the anger and frustration we are experiencing in the workplace comes home with us. And we are not even aware how it got in the front door. It's important, then, in dealing with your anger, to explore the role the stress known as burnout is playing in your current situation.

Who Gets Burned Out?

Many different types of people can be at risk of burning out. It's not just the "A" type superachievers who are at risk—although they are certainly high on the "at risk" list. Others on the list include people who heard a lot of those funky little shoulds from their parents. Specifically at risk are people who were indoctrinated with the type of shoulds that provided them with impossibly high standards or shoulds that addressed their achievement, perfection, competence, and tenacity. Parental talk like, "Whatever you start, you should stick with and finish," or adages like, "There's no point in doing something unless you do it right," can really make people feel lousy if they don't measure up.

Another group of people at risk for burnout are those in the helping professions, such as nursing, social work, teaching, ministry, or counseling. In many of these professions, the pay is quite low considering the scope of the work. With the exception of nursing and certain other segments of specific professions, many of these professionals are regulated by bureaucracies or by government entities that make getting things done more tedious and individual recognition hard to come by.

The population many of these people deal with is usually a needy one. After awhile, rather than feeling the joy and satisfaction of helping others, many individuals in the helping professions experience the frustration of working against impossible odds, while carrying bottomless responsibility. Often times they have to bear the burden of failure. Many of the people within the populations who come for help are ready to take what they need from the person working with them and then move on without providing their "helper" with any type of positive reinforcement. The helpers never get the chance to discover if what they are doing has mattered in any significant way. It's no wonder so many people working in the helping professions feel so unappreciated and angry that they eventually burnout and leave their professions because they end up believing what they do is really a meaningless and thankless task.

Another segment of the population that suffers from burnout consists of regular people who work in large bureaucracies. You can probably understand how this could be the case. Large business entities become stratified and anonymous. Within bureaucracies, there's no room for personal achievement, and mediocrity is fostered. Rules and regulations do not allow for the growth of the individual. There are no rewards for novel concepts and solutions, and thus, as with the helping professions, there is little chance for personal positive reinforcement. People become discouraged and disgruntled and eventually may give up trying to be creative.

People with charisma also can easily become victims of burnout due to the expectations of other people. Charismatic people possess a certain type of magnetism that attracts people to them. Other people just plain feel good around people with charisma, and others attribute all sorts of abilities to charismatic people. Always expected to shine, to do more, and to be better than everyone else, these charming people burn out trying to live up to those unrealistic expectations.

A final category of people at risk for burnout and the anger it produces includes just about *everybody else*. People who are goal oriented, idealistic, dedicated, tenacious, and talented make great candidates. Burnout can affect anyone who is committed to what he or she undertakes.

The following exercise will help you think about where you fall on the burnout continuum. Are you getting what you need from your job? Is your career providing you with adequate challenges and rewards? Take a minute to think about how your shoulds are affecting your work. Look for any family of origin principles that mediate the way you behave in the workplace. Look for messages from the past about the way "We" do things.

EXERCISE
How My Shoulds Affect My Work

Examine principles such as: "We put the family first" or "We sacrifice everything for the job" or "We don't trust outsiders to do it right." Jot down any principles that may be operating on your present behavior and may be causing you problems.

_____

_____

_____

Look back for any family myths that might be affecting you. These myths could include items like, "Old papa was a poor immigrant who never gave up trying" or, "Grandmother single-handedly held off three robbers and saved the family fortune." How have these myths affected your attitude or behavior?

_____

_____

_____

Family principles and myths can cause us to attempt to behave in unrealistic ways that can also contribute to burnout and subsequently to self-angering. Once again, in protecting ourselves and taking care of our needs, awareness that something isn't right or that something just feels wrong is the first step toward good management.

Red Flags for Burnout

There are several red flags for diagnosing burnout in yourself or in a loved one. And, because burnout results

117

from stress, you'll notice that many of the red flags for burnout are the same as the symptoms of stress. See if any of these symptoms of burnout apply to you or someone you love:

- Has anybody mentioned that you or a loved one seems stressed? Listen to family members or others you know care about you or your loved one when they voice their concerns.
- Do you or a loved one have the four Ds—disengagement, distancing, dulling, and deadness?
- Have you noticed that you or a loved one seems more remote than is usual?
- Do you or a loved one appear uninterested in doing things you formerly enjoyed?
- Do you or a loved one seem to be unable to focus as well as you normally can?
- Have you noticed yourself or a loved one displaying a flat affect; that is, your mood seems to lack its normal little ups and downs?
- Have you or a loved one lost direction? Are actions you take directed at a goal or just action for action sake? If there is no goal behind the action, you may have lost your direction.
- Do you or your loved one seem to have lost interest in life? Does life energize or deplete you? Are you involved or detached? Are you feeling enthusiastic or cynical? Do you feel you have a purpose in life or are you just wasting time?
- Do you or a loved one deny your situation in life? Failure to examine reality can be dangerous to yourself and others.

- Have you or a loved one become uncaring toward others? Someone who is stressed out may not take adequate care of him- or herself and may be thoughtless in regard to others.
- Do you or a loved one show signs of clinical depression? If you are depressed, disoriented, and paranoid, you should seek professional help. These are serious symptoms and more than just simple burnout.

Basically, burnout results from anger and frustration over unrealized hopes and dreams.

Smokey the Bear

As Smokey always told us, "Only you can prevent forest fires," and the same goes for personal burnout. Only you can combat it. Once you know the red flags, you'll be ready to take charge and combat burnout. You obviously can't quit working, but there are things that you can do to add some zip to your life.

Communication is important in combating your burnout for a number of reasons. Even if the workplace provides you with little reinforcement or too much stress, having a close confidant you can talk with about the situation can take the edge off the problem. Just getting some feedback is good. Sometimes just hearing somebody say you're not going crazy or that you're doing a good job can be quite helpful. Also, in sharing your disappointment or frustration with another human being, you unload some of the negative energy that depletes your spirit.

If you didn't get the credit you felt you deserved at work and you're feeling a little angry or disappointed about it, don't just suck it up. It will just add to your resentment and fuel your burnout. Try to find someone with whom you can share your feelings. It will help.

Humans work best and are most productive when they work in small groups. If you work in a bureaucracy, see if there is any way you can interact with a few other people who are working on the same type of thing as you are. Reach out for connections in any place that you can. Colleagues who work on faceless, splintered, monster projects become so stratified that even when they are told what's up, they may not understand what's going on. They may not ever feel like they fit in. They are likely to feel their work is irrelevant.

It's one thing to feel like a cog in a wheel, but it's ultimately more devastating not even to know where the wheel is heading. Without having a destination or a sense of completion or achievement, it's impossible to feel pride in what you are doing. You'll learn more about what's going on if you can collaborate, even if it's only one little snippet at a time. Each person can then help consolidate the acquired information.

When you have more information about what's happening, you'll feel more in control and more a part of things. You will perhaps gain some insight into the "big picture." This, then, can provide you with a better understanding of your particular bureaucracy's goal. You'll then have a better idea of what your organization is ultimately trying to achieve. With this in mind, you'll have rationale for what you are doing. Having such a rationale can help provide your job with more meaning.

Here's another thing to remember about bureaucracies. The more competent the worker, the more the worker is at risk for developing an "I don't care" attitude. This type of apathy is functional burnout generated by the system itself. The larger the organization, the greater the tendency for the organization to place more emphasis on the appearance or outward signs of work than on the actual work itself.

This situation means there's bound to be a lot of pencil pushing and micromanaging going on. This pseudo-efficiency can have a very negative effect on individuals who consider themselves to be self-motivated self-starters or entrepreneurs. Such a job culture presents a competent person with a serious double-bind. If he ignores the system, its logbooks, and its checks and double checks, and just goes ahead and does the work he's supposed to do, he exposes himself to two dangers. First, he may be seen by cohorts as uncooperative and not a team player. They may "dis" him. Secondly, if he decides to go along with the gag, he'll probably find himself engaged day after day in a seemingly endless supply of meaningless paperwork and red tape. This predicament is a guaranteed recipe for burnout.

Bureaucracies are a wonderful place to observe the Peter Principle in action. Because bureaucracies tend to have job ceilings, a Catch-22 for sure, competent people may be passed over for promotions. Imaginative people simply don't fit very well into bureaucracies. Subsequently, incompetence rises. Colorless or politically oriented bureaucrats tend to do well and climb the ladder. This creates a conundrum for the more motivated people—should they work under an inferior, someone who is less motivated to achieve than they are, or leave the system? Rugged individualists get angry, give up, and tend to leave rather than stay in positions where they believe they are inadequately compensated.

Bureaucracies aren't the only hot beds of burnout. Regular office situations can have their pitfalls, as well, for a couple of reasons:

1. The organizational structure of a particular corporate environment can produce burnout.
2. Certain personality characteristics of people attracted to certain businesses can create their own burnout. Frequently, perfectionists are attracted to careers that place unceasing and unachievable demands upon them.

The goal of most all organizations is to put the interests of the organization in the forefront. Why have a company if not to produce something? It's just the nature of the beast. So, even if the organization isn't a bureaucracy, it still is a self-perpetuating machine with its own self-interests at the top of the agenda.

One out of ten people suffer from anger-producing burnout in the workplace, so it's a good idea to take a look at some of the forces at work creating it. If you believe you may be at risk, consider the following issues and see how your work situation measures up. If your job doesn't measure up, think about what you might be able to do to improve the situation. People are at less risk of burnout in organizations that are attentive to the following issues:

- People experience a better attitude in companies that provide their employees with a sense of personal responsibility for the company's fate. Employees want to feel as though they are making a meaningful contribution to the company.

- Workers suffer from less burnout in businesses that offer salaries that are appropriate and commensurate with the work being done.
- Companies that can offer advancement opportunities to employees report lower burnout than those companies that set ceilings.
- Companies that provide their workers with feedback—both negative and positive—are more comfortable workplaces. People need to know how they're doing, and they need to know when they are appreciated.
- Companies that provide their employees with clear job descriptions and companies that guide rather than dictate to their employees create fewer burnt-out workers.
- Companies that provide their employees with a good understanding of the corporate vision and those that can negotiate flextime schedules are less stress- and anger-provoking environments in which to work.
- Companies that offer challenge and choice encourage professional and personal growth and give employees a chance at succeeding. People who enjoy a challenge do well in this type of environment. They are not pigeonholed into rigid ways of performing their tasks. Companies that achieve this type of business climate are not likely to micromanage their employees to death.

In addition, there are certain personal traits that burnout-hardy people possess that help insulate them:

- Workers who can focus have the ability to see their varied tasks through to completion. They don't get sidetracked by e-mails, unforeseen demands, and irrelevant meetings. They tend to have clear expectations of what needs to be accomplished and what can be accomplished, and don't place unreasonable demands upon themselves. While focus is a personality trait, it is best achieved in an environment that allows employees to stay on task and does not insist on unreasonable demands.

- Employees who have energy to get the work done are much more productive. Being more productive, they feel good about what they accomplish and have good self-esteem that shows through in what they do. Energy is a personality trait, but organizations can go a long way to enhance those traits by furnishing employees with challenges and choices.

- Productive workers know how to reenergize themselves. They find ways to reduce their stress levels through stress management techniques such as exercise, meditation, hobbies, and social support networks. (Chapter 8 contains many examples of these techniques.) By conserving and restoring their energy, productive employees keep themselves from becoming discouraged, overwhelmed, and disengaged. Disengagement can lead to anger, anxiety, uncertainty, frustration, and alienation, and job performance will suffer. An apathetic attitude can sabotage the chance of getting any rewards that might keep an employee interested in work and happy with him- or herself.

- People who are happy in their work situation don't procrastinate. Oftentimes, people procrastinate because they feel insecure or because they fear that they're likely to fail at something. This is a setup for more failure. The more someone procrastinates, the more likely that she'll run out of time to do a good, or even adequate, job and she will indeed fail at what she's trying to accomplish. Failures are the seeds for growing more insecurity!

- People who are comfortable in their jobs can concentrate and avoid distractions. Distraction is another setup for problems because distraction leads to mistakes due to a lack of concentration on the task at hand. Some organizations unfortunately amplify this tendency toward distraction by encouraging or demanding frenetic activity. Watch out!

Your Own Worst Enemy

Finally, due to their personality styles, certain individuals are just plain at higher risk for burnout than others. Top performers who work in fast-paced, demanding businesses are especially at risk. Frequently, that type of aggressive environment is just the kind of place in which many of these people find themselves employed. Paradoxically, peak performers can create their own systems that can lead to stress and anger.

High performers with strong self-management skills require little supervision. They are usually counted on to know what to do and how to do it. The downside of having these admirable traits is that, for these folks, successes can become a drug. These individuals develop a "tolerance" for their stressful workloads and require more and more projects and more and more successes to get a "fix."

Successful people can be their own worst enemies by

125

believing they'll feel better about everything and able to relax if they can just finish that one project or make one more big sale. They reach their goal and then the high wears off. They start all over again, only they need higher levels of work and challenge to obtain the desired effect. The more they succeed, the more they need to succeed— achievement becomes its own reward. It's not surprising that managers tend to heap never-ending projects on the neutron star employees. Eventually they'll destroy themselves trying to reach new goals. They'll go supernova. Burnout can occur for these individuals when a nagging little fear creeps in and whispers that they can't achieve more and the jig is up. They may then disengage or become depressed and cynical and even resist taking on new challenges.

If any of this feels a little familiar and you're not likely to change your career, it may be time to make a few changes in your life to compensate. Some good old stress management tips can help.

7

Stress:
Its Effects on Your Anger and Your Health

It's now known that stress bears a relationship to not only our emotional state, but also to our physical health as well. Research established this connection by focusing on the measurement of endocrine responses in bodies under stress. One model for what happens to the body when stressed is the general adaptation syndrome.

The hallmark of this theory is its three-stage model of stress that includes the alarm stage, the stress resistance stage, and the exhaustion stage. In the alarm stage, the "flight or fight" response, which was discussed in the Chapter 1, again puts in an appearance. Just as it does when you get angry, this automatic arousal mechanism prepares your body for whatever may come next. As we know, this response is highly adaptive and crucial for our survival. Thanks to your body's sympathetic nervous system, when what is perceived as a threatening stressor occurs, your body automatically prepares to face it.

The stress resistance stage occurs after the immediate threat disappears. Your body relaxes slightly, but it still continues to stay mobilized for action as stress hormones, like adrenalin and cortisol, continue to be released into your body. Vigilance remains increased, and your body is still scanning in a "just in case" fashion.

Finally, if the stress level stays high, your body enters

the exhaustion stage. After long or repeated exposure to stress, your body's adaptive energy capacity becomes exhausted. It just gets zapped. It is at this point that you can experience lowered immunity or a tendency toward accidents, bad judgment, and anger blowups.

Here's a practical example of how the general adaptation syndrome works. Say you just avoided a near collision (the alarm stage). You had to swerve like crazy and do some fancy brakework, but it looks like the guy who nearly creamed you is well out of the way. You may notice that your heart is pounding in your ears. Also, you are aware that your right leg and right foot are still shaking. You sigh, your eyes keep finding the rearview mirror, and you glance left and right.

You are now at the resistance stage of stress. If you were to remain in this state, you could enter the exhaustion stage and you might end up with a terrible headache, leg cramps, and who knows what else. It's possible that you'd feel so goofed up and so cranky that you'd do something really stupid.

Right Brain/Left Brain—It's Not a Tossup

It is thought by some researchers that early man probably didn't differentiate between himself and the "other" very well. He had no conscious awareness of "I" versus "it." Everything was part of nature; everything was part of everything else. Man was just one aspect of a world and a sky that were full of magic and mystery. However, nowadays we do differentiate between "me" and "you" and "it." We are also aware that the brain's two hemispheres are responsible for different functions and that in order to

129

function properly as whole beings, we need to use both.

Some research suggests that around 3,000 years ago, or maybe back even a bit further in time, man became *self-aware*. He became aware of himself as an entity apart from other things. He began to develop *consciousness*. This self-awareness helped him begin to see that his "essence" was not the same as his nose or foot. The French philosopher Rene Descartes described this distinction when he made his famous statement, "I think, therefore I am."

Much of the time we operate in what's known as a right-brain mode. The right brain provides us with a holistic, integrated, relaxed look at the world. Unlike the right brain, the left brain is more concerned with focusing on the here and now: It works in a more linear way, more like a computer. When you learn a task, your left brain is quite active and aware. For example, if you ever took tennis lessons, you may remember what it was like.

You had to be aware of where all your body parts were at once. Not only did you have to keep your eye on the ball, you had to be concerned with how far away you were from it and whether you were perpendicular to it. You had to think about where your feet were and if your backhand had follow-through. Then, hopefully, as you learned more, you allowed your right brain to get in there, too, and you relaxed—and your game improved.

Learning to drive presents another example. When you were first learning this skill, you were aware of everything. You kept your eye on the old guy with the white hair and the floppy green hat getting ready to cross the street. You noticed he had a cane. In a nanosecond you speculated on whether or not he would trip in front of your car when you passed through the intersection. You checked the speed you were traveling. You were aware that "Hey Jude" was playing on the radio. You gauged the yellow light at the corner, analyzing things, to see if you could make it. You saw the cop sitting at the corner to the left. You figured you'd better not chance making it through the yellow and got ready to stop for the red.

When you first learned to drive, these threads of information were things you were consciously aware of seeing or hearing on an individual basis. You were using your left brain. As your skills developed, you made the shift to a more relaxed driving style and the individual pieces wove themselves together, becoming part of an integrated "fabric" of the driving task. Driving now, operating primarily with your right brain, you still are conscious of everything and all the facts are still available if they're needed, but you are aware on a different level. This frees you to an extent to ruminate on what you're going to have for dinner or on whether or not to see a movie on Friday night. When threat arises, however, you revert to the other type of processing, utilizing more of your left-brain capacities, focusing on relevant and crucial facts for dealing with critical situations. It becomes a "me against them" situation. It's the survival instinct. It's appropriate and necessary, but it's tiring. In fact, if you stay that way, you wind up pooped.

The Relation of Stress Resistance to Anger

The stress resistance stage also works on an interpersonal level. Suppose you are having problems at home. Here you are, in front of your house after a bad day at work or school. As you ready yourself to open your front door—

because of what's been going on—your left-brain scanner activates. You're ready for trouble. Perhaps you're even rehearsing different defensive strategies in response to any of several different conflict scenarios that you anticipate could unfold.

Because you're late, you figure your husband is going to grill you about where you've been. You expect he'll probably complain that dinner isn't ready, too, or that you didn't get all the clothes folded and put away. So, before he gets on you, you decide you'll remind him up front that he keeps forgetting to fix the broken sprinkler and never remembers to take out the trash.

You enter the house and find him in the kitchen preparing dinner. Aroused and ready to interpret nuances of even the most innocuous events in a negative or threatening way, you may actually be responsible for what's known as a "self-fulfilling prophecy." You've front-loaded yourself. Armed for bear, you don't read the situation correctly, and you overreact. Oh great, you think, your husband never cooks. You just know he's mad. Figuring that the best defense is a good offense, you start to tell him all his faults. He feels like he's being attacked. All he was trying to do was surprise you with a couple of steaks. His feelings are hurt, but instead of saying so, he blows up, throws the frying pan, and stomps off to the garage.

Basically, you mishandled the situation due to your frame of mind and incorrect interpretations. Or you wind up blowing it because of the way you adapted your behavior to meet what you perceived to be a negatively loaded situation. So, you only added to your stress level, but may have actually caused the situation you wanted to avoid, a confrontation. And you may not even be aware of your part in it!

Your Body and Mind Under Siege

Unfortunately, the more these types of stressors occur, the more likely you are to put yourself at risk not only for anger, but also for illness and accidents. Your body reacts to stress both physiologically and psychologically. Maybe you've experienced this phenomenon when, for instance, after a prolonged period of stress, things finally seem to lighten up and *then* you come down with a cold. A stressed-out body is likely to suffer lowered immunity to disease and be more prone to anger.

In your body's attempts to prepare for stressful situations, it reverts to the same coping mechanisms our ancestors called into action for a quick dash across the plains. You experience automatic physiologic responses that are great for short-term threats, but leave you trashed over the long haul.

How Long-Term Physiologic Stress Affects Your Body

Muscle tension is fabulous when quick reaction times are important, but over time, strain can lead to cramps and muscle-induced tension headaches. Breathing increases that serve to supply more oxygen for rapid bursts of energy and quick thinking can lead to problems with hyperventilation and, ultimately, blackouts. Under stress, digestion is interrupted or stops altogether. Your bowel can be affected, too. Need I say how? The problem is, if you're under a great deal of unremitting stress, you're continually invoking your body's stress response, which can lead to digestive problems like ulcers, indigestion, spastic colon, and colitis.

Hearts work overtime under stress. The relationship between chronic anger and heart attack is now virtually accepted. Noted physicians like Andrew Weil and Dean Ornish teach stress-management techniques to their patients to help them avoid further problems. Hypertension is also a real problem for many people in the United States. Stress increases red corpuscles, which can result in clots in the bloodstream. Management of high blood pressure can include medication, attention to diet, life-style changes, and reducing stress.

Psychological Effects of Stress

When you're stressed, you may begin to notice certain psychological symptoms such as these:

- Minor problems throw you off or seem insurmountable; you may notice that even little things really bother you, or that little things seem overwhelming.
- Tasks that once were easy may become onerous and you might have trouble concentrating.
- Being around people may feel threatening because you may feel distrustful of others. Former friends may not be coming around much and seem evasive.
- You may believe there's no one you can talk to or that you're trapped in your predicament with no way out.
- You may find that you're always thinking about your problems, ruminating on them to the exclusion of other things. This preoccupation can ultimately lead to accidents and bad decisions. If you're not taking care of business in the here and now, you become accident prone.
- Formerly fun activities, like sex and eating, may no longer bring you any pleasure or become distasteful.

This inability to feel pleasure is called anhedonia, and it's not good.

- You may be having a hard time getting along with other people or feel fatigued and exhausted. You may be getting into fights.
- At work or school or in social interactions, you may have noticed that your productivity is down. Others might have commented on it.
- You may notice that you're not sleeping as well as you once did or that you're sleeping all the time.
- Maybe you caught yourself eating too much or too little or drinking or smoking when you never did before.

If any of these symptoms sound familiar, don't be surprised; you're reacting to stress. We all do, in different ways and to different degrees. When stress manifests as anger or when physical or psychological symptoms become chronic and zap your quality of life or become threatening, it's time to take another look at what's going on and seek some outside help. Your stress may have pushed you to the edge of an anxiety disorder or clinical depression.

Generally speaking, becoming aware of your problematic situations, being willing to look at yourself nondefensively, and being open to change can work little miracles. To see how you're coping with stress in your life, try the following exercise. It's a list of negative thoughts that pop into everybody's head, and in this exercise you rate how frequently they pop into yours. Your score will tell you how well you cope with stress.

EXERCISE
How I Cope with Stress

Check any thought you had over the last week, then indicate how frequently it occurred, assigning a value of 1 through 5 for each one. Remember, everyone has negative self-thoughts sometimes!

Not at All = 0
Almost Never = 1
Moderately Often = 2
Often = 3
Constantly = 4

1. I'm no good. ○ _____

2. I can't get things together. ○ _____

3. I'm a failure. ○ _____

4. I wish I were a kinder person. ○ _1_

5. I hate myself. ○ _____

6. My life is a mess. ○ _____

7. I can't seem to finish anything I start. ○ _____

8. I know I'm weak. ○ _____

9. There is probably something wrong with me. ○ _____

10. I'm a loser. ○ _____

11. No one lets me succeed. ○ _____

12. I can't get motivated. ○ _____

13. I keep letting people down. ○ _____

14. I feel out of control. ○ _○_

15. Nothing feels like fun anymore. ○ _○_

16. Nobody understands me. ○ _○_

17. Nobody supports me. ○ _○_

18. I'm not a lovable person. ○ _1_

19. I wish I could just disappear from here. ○ _○_

20. Everyone is against me. ○ _○_

Total score: _3_

If you scored 30 or under, you're handling stress pretty well. If you scored above 30, take a look at the areas that are causing you the most discomfort. It's those negative thoughts you'll want to focus on first.

Time Is of the Essence

Over the years there's been a debate about how two different personality types, dubbed "A" and "B," fared when it came to anger and stress. Originally identified by two cardiologists, the people with these personalities were supposed to have quite different ways of dealing with anger, stress, and life in general.

Type A Personality

Type A people are described as overly competitive, impatient, and easily frustrated They are said to be hard on themselves and overly critical of others. In conversation,

A's tend to talk quickly and hurry conversations. If they think you're speaking too slowly, they may finish sentences for you. A's supposedly also move quickly, try to do more than one thing at a time, and love to be involved in multiple jobs with multiple deadlines. A's are always conscious of the time—in fact, they're overly conscious of it. A's never are late, and, indeed, they are likely to be early. They are always trying to better themselves. Not surprisingly they are, for the most part, the world's overachievers.

Originally it was believed that A's made up the majority of the world's heart-attack patients. Later research on the subject suggests it's not so much the Type A style itself that leads to a heart attack, but that Type A people *who are chronically angry* are at risk.

Type B Personality

Type B personalities, on the other hand, are, well, let's just say they're the opposite of the A's. They're described as laid back and much more *stress tolerant*. B's don't worry if they're late—so what, it's no big deal. If the baby has a little poopy in his diapers, the B will get around to changing him, eventually. As you might well guess (especially if you see in yourself some A tendencies), B's could make the A's crazy.

Managing Anger: Type A vs. Type B

The A/B personality hypothesis is worth considering when it comes to anger and self-management. Remember that anger managers use problem situations as opportunities for constructive change. People can certainly be a mixture of both Type A and Type B in different situations, but those with more high-strung personality styles are more easily aroused. So, if you find that you have more A than

B in you, it behooves you to examine your behavior to determine if you are placing yourself at risk for self-angering situations. If this is the case, you can take control and provide yourself with escape hatches to avoid these situations.

If you find that you are an A, take some time to discover what areas are problems for you, and think about ways you can get what you need without becoming annoyed or angry and without turning off those around you. For instance, if you're an A, take that into consideration in transactions with other people. Do you arrive at places early and then feel totally frustrated and angry that no one else is there yet and you're wasting your time? Since it's probably impossible for you to make yourself be late or even on time, bring a book with you, take a project to work on, file your nails, or organize your Palm Pilot. You have to play the cards you're dealt, after all.

If you're an A, some of the situations like the examples that follow might cause you problems. Feeling as though it's the principle of the thing, you may try to tough it out. Or you may feel almost compelled to do things the way you always do them, when with a little creative problem solving, you could either avoid what bugs you or at least defuse the impact upon you. To help you think about how you can avoid or defuse the impact of circumstances that normally aggravate you, read the following problems and consider the obvious solutions recommended for keeping you on an even keel:

- **Problem 1:** It's Saturday afternoon and you're at the mall. You know there is never anyplace to park and you know wasting your time driving around in circles makes you angry. Obvious solutions:

a. Try going early (or late) on a Monday.
b. Shop online.
c. Use the phone.

- **Problem 2:** You're headed out to get the newspaper and that annoying neighbor who talks on and on and complains about everything is down at the curb. Obvious solutions:

a. Wait to get the paper.
b. Have your spouse go for you.
c. Train the dog to do it.

- **Problem 3:** You're forced to sit in unending traffic on the highway. It's brutal; it drives you crazy. Obvious solutions:

a. Take another route, even if it takes a bit longer.
b. Try going at a different time.
c. Try using books on tape to keep your mind off the waiting.

- **Problem 4:** You've decided to go back to school, you put off writing your final paper until the night before it's due, and now your child has started throwing up. Obvious solutions:

a. Arrange for backup help in advance.
b. Learn new ways to prioritize.
c. Complete assignments as soon as they are assigned.

Time Management Techniques to the Rescue

Whether you're a Type A or Type B, a few time management ideas will help you feel less stressed out and less angry and pressured. An easy way to visualize a time management model is by picturing a series of drawers. In the top drawer go things that need immediate attention. The second drawer contains things that will need to be dealt with very soon. The third drawer holds items that will have to be dealt with eventually. The bottom drawer is for things you'll probably never get around to. You may already be familiar with the time management chest of drawers model. It's a classic.

Time Management Model

The Four Boxes of Time

Somewhat like the time management chest is another useful time management tool. I call the model the Four Boxes of Time. It looks like this.

Four Boxes of Time

By using this model, you can divide your waking hours more appropriately, which will enable you to prioritize things in order of their importance.

Box One: Critical Things

In this box are things that are crucial to your life— things that could lead to disaster if put off, such as necessary surgery, funerals, important money matters, and so on. Many people operate out of this box helter-skelter, which leads to constantly putting out fires. They never seem to have a chance to take things as they come. For them life is an angering, continually looming disaster. If you believe you are operating primarily out of the first compartment, you should probably take a step back and reevaluate your priorities. To maximize your time management, do your best to keep the first box as clear as possible, but remember, life does happen and you'll wind up with stuff in there whether you want it or not.

Box Two: Soon-to-Be Critical Things

In the second box are things that are important, but not yet critical. These might be things like next month's house payment bill or remembering that the kids need their shots or that you need to renew your driver's license next month. Be careful! If not managed, items in box two can become critical!

Box Three: Normal Things

The third box contains things that should get done eventually or they'll probably wind up in the second box. This box could hold magazine subscriptions you might like to renew, appointments you'll want to make eventually, things that aren't imminently important. You're ultimate goal is to keep yourself operating in boxes two and three. In these areas you are able to take care of things as they come along, not allowing unfinished business to become catastrophic.

Box Four: Unimportant Things

In the final box are things that really can be put off, such as organizing coupons, cleaning out the garage,

143

learning how to burn CDs, writing to Aunt Ethel, and stuff like that. Attend to issues in box four when you have time or are really, really bored.

Finding Balance

In order to live in a healthy way and keep ourselves from becoming stressed out and overwhelmed, we need to provide ourselves with the time to nurture three aspects of life. To achieve balance, we need to make time for work, for leisure, and for learning. The time spent in each of these areas ebbs and flows over the course of our lifetime.

As little kids, we overlap the three aspects quite a bit, and they are rather blurred. Leisure, or play, is the main

Balance Wheel, Childhood

component, but within the area of play, a bunch of learning takes place and so does a lot of work. As children grow a little older, the areas become more clearly defined. Learning takes the shape of schooling and work may take the form of chores.

The focus changes somewhat as we become adults and the work area of life gains true ascendance. For many people at this stage of life, the learning area becomes secondary or nonexistent, and the leisure area may be sacrificed to enhance the more critical work area. Work, it's true, is a very necessary part of adulthood. But many people sacrifice balance in its service, and to do so can produce stress. All work and no play makes Jack a dull—and possibly angry—boy.

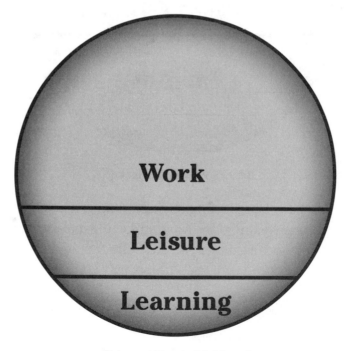

Balance Wheel, Adulthood

145

As middle age approaches, many people, if they are fortunate and if they work at it, experience a renaissance in the leisure and learning areas of their lives. As their commitment to traditional forms of work diminishes, they have the time to rebalance their priorities.

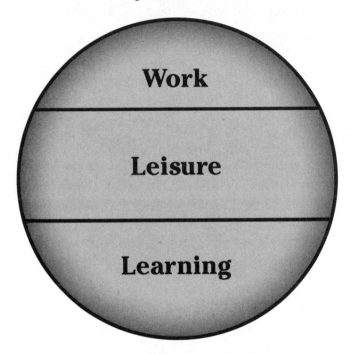

Balance Wheel, Middle Age

If you have been feeling stressed out, overwhelmed, or angry, you may want to see how well you're balancing your time. Your priorities may need a bit of a tune-up.

8

Stress-Survival Techniques

Hardiness

Finally, there is some *good news* regarding stress and anger. There are many things that can help you help yourself when it comes to managing you external stressors. Some years ago, researchers who thought about such things began to wonder why it was that certain sets of people did better under stress, stayed healthier, and suffered less severe consequences than others, even though they both may have been subjected to the same hellish situations. Social scientists looked at people who had been in concentration camps and people who had been prisoners of war and such. Eventually, certain similarities or character traits began to emerge that the successful survivors seemed to have in common. The scientists wondered how these specific proclivities insulated these people from otherwise overwhelming situations.

Here's the good news. Even if you don't currently have these stress shields built into your personality structure, you can acquire them. You can start by simply becoming aware of them and then adding the traits to your behavioral repertoire. In no time you'll strengthen your ability to handle stress and pressure.

Let's go over a few of them.

Spirituality

People who do well under stress appear to possess a sense of spirituality. This does not necessarily mean they are religious, although that certainly could be. The stress-resilient people share a feeling of wholeness or a sense of relationship with the universe. They have a sense of belonging to something greater than themselves. Whether this feeling of spirituality is something that occurs when these folks are in church or whether it happens while they are lying under a tree picking dandelions from sun-dappled grass, doesn't make a difference. Perhaps this spirituality has something of a peak experience about it. People experiencing this state of consciousness frequently report that time seems to stop and everything is accepted and understood if just for a brief second.

Humor

A sense of humor is also an important coping tactic and hardiness factor. Not taking yourself too seriously definitely helps. A good sense of humor keeps you from giving up your power and energy to problems and to people who are, in the ultimate scheme of things, not going to change the earth's orbit. Seeing the human condition in your situation can sometimes provide perspective.

Creativity

People who are resistant think creatively. They have the ability to look at things in unusual ways. My favorite example of this comes from a *Star Trek* movie, *Star Trek II— The Wrath of Khan*. Woven into the plot line is a theme where Admiral Kirk is asked over and over how he was able to succeed at solving an unbeatable problem, the "Kobayashi

Maru," during his days as a cadet at the Starfleet Academy. Finally, in answer to all the queries put to him about how he did it, Kirk states simply that he changed the setup for the test, allowing for success. Simply put, he says, "I cheated."

Another example comes from ancient stories about Alexander the Great. There was a legend that whoever could untie the "Gordion Knot" would rule all of Asia Minor. Undaunted, Alexander undid it. Well, technically anyway, he severed the annoying knot with his sword.

This is not to recommend cheating or sword wielding; it just means that sometimes "outside of the box" thinking can be useful, and sometimes problems are best solved in unusual or creative ways.

Independence

Stress-resistant people appear to be independent. They measure their worth by their own standards and do not rely on the opinion of other people. They possess a positive attitude and a sense that it all will come out in the wash. You can see how many of these traits fortify one another. It's probable that the more confident you feel, the more successful you will be. The more successes you achieve, the higher your sense of accomplishment, self-efficacy, and ultimately, self-esteem.

Support

Another fact that the research turned up was that hardy people have good support groups. A church group, a bunch of friends to ride bikes with, or a car club may serve as a support group. It's now a well-established fact that support groups can play a major role in the survival rates of heart and cancer recovery patients.

Passion

The researchers also pointed out the importance of hobbies and passions in the lives of the resilient group. The renowned mythologist Joseph Campbell agreed. He taught us we must "follow our bliss." He urged people to find something they truly loved and do it! In losing yourself to your passion—playing sports, gardening, pursuing the arts, doing whatever you love—you can help reduce your stress level.

Have you ever noticed, when you ask someone how it was that she played such a fabulous game of tennis, closed a great deal, or got an A on a paper, what she says? Typically, she'll tell you she really doesn't know. She'll say she felt as if she were "right on" and that looking back, whatever she did just seemed to come naturally and very easily. Passions and hobbies help you get in sync, and things that formerly drove you crazy become insignificant.

Self-Esteem

At the root of hardiness is, perhaps, a good sense of self-esteem. What are the hallmarks of self-esteem?

- Surrounding yourself with people who nurture you
- Becoming you own approving inner parent
- Trusting yourself
- Making your own rules in a responsible fashion
- Following your own intuition
- Letting yourself win and not feeling guilty
- Surrounding yourself with beauty
- Giving yourself pleasure without feeling guilty about it
- Having fun responsibly without guilt

- Rewarding yourself
- Having confidence in your abilities
- Creating an abundance of friends
- Replacing negative self-talk with gentle, loving self-talk
- Developing your creativity

It is important that you as an individual possess adequate self-esteem because your level of self-worth can help you improve your circumstances, and help you to stay in charge of your reactions to others and to life in general.

Generally self-esteem problems fall into one of two categories:

1. **Situational self-esteem problems.** These issues show up only some of the time and only under certain specific conditions. These self-worth problems may involve some type of cognitive distortion that deals with body image or perceived deficits in other areas. These problems can be greatly improved by practice in disputing them.

2. **Character logical self-esteem problems.** These issues, on the other hand, are concerned with more basic and global identity issues like feeling as if you're a worthless or stupid person, or a loser, or you're just plain feeling "bad." Improvement in these areas can come about by focusing your attention on self-compassion and nonjudgmental beliefs and affirmations. Some other techniques that are helpful in improving this type of self-esteem problem are the use of visualizations and hypnotic trance techniques. You'll hear more about these techniques later in this chapter.

You'd probably agree that everyone occasionally succumbs to negative thinking patterns and everyone has a critical inner voice. Well, the person with feelings of poor self-worth has got it much worse. His hot thoughts take the form of a pathologically negative self-sabotaging critic. If you're a person with low self-esteem, your self-critic is likely to set you up with impossibly high standards and then beat you up for even trying to attain them. Your self-critic tells you that you have to be the best, then calls you names and makes you believe that the names are true. It exaggerates bad things and uses many different weapons. Your self-critic is fond of using the rules you grew up with because the critic is born in your childhood and knows your mom and dad.

There are four factors that will dictate how your childhood self-esteem was affected:

1. The degree to which your tastes were labeled good or bad
2. The degree to which your parents were able to differentiate between you and your behavior
3. The frequency of negative messages your parents sent you
4. The frequency with which you were subjected to negative gestures that were tied to rejection

As an adult you can choose to live with your negative childhood critic or disarm it. At the root of self-esteem is having compassion for yourself.

First of all, you have to be able to understand your issues and problems. This doesn't necessarily mean that you have to find solutions for them, but merely that you become aware they exist. It means you must figure out how you operate in the world and what you are likely to do in varied situations. You need to have an idea of where you're coming from.

Next, in order to develop compassion for yourself, you need to learn how to accept yourself—all of yourself—even with your perceived shortcomings. This is how the process of change can begin. Accept who you are and don't beat yourself up, even though it's not so easy! But you're a hero, actually. You carry on in spite of everything that goes wrong. The degree of your success is irrelevant; the only thing that really counts is the effort. With that thought in mind comes acceptance.

Lastly, for compassion to come about, you'll want to forgive yourself. The ability to forgive yourself and others stems from your self-understanding and self-acceptance. Now, this doesn't mean you have to approve of every-thing about yourself and everything you've ever done. But the future is a clean slate on which many things can be written. Letting go of the past and its mistakes and dis-appointments frees up your energy to discover new ways of thinking and behaving. It's quite wonderful, really, when you can achieve this compassionate frame of mind!

If you currently don't have good self-esteem—nurture it. There are piles of things that can help. One good way to begin to build your sense of self-esteem and mastery is by practicing positive self-statements. Practice this in the fol-lowing exercise.

EXERCISE
Making Positive Self-Statements

Look at the list of adjectives below. First, place a check next to each word that describes you at work. Next, underline any word that applies to you when you're with your partner or spouse. Last, circle any word that describes you when you're alone. Don't be modest!

generous	good	independent ✓
talkative	tolerant	efficient ✓
warm	willing to learn	confident ✓
reliable	cooperative	persistent ✓
fun to be around	trustworthy ✓	handy
adventurous	serious ✓	dexterous
bold ✓	easygoing	sweet
supportive	quiet	competitive ✓
dependable ✓	content	people like me
zany	secure	positive ✓
enterprising ✓	satisfied with myself	humble
helpful	achieving ✓	tactful
kind	useful	resourceful ✓
self-assured ✓	accomplished	amiable
sincere ✓	polite	happy
cool	active ✓	stable
hard working	determined ✓	spiritual
loving	creative	humorous ✓
consistent	relaxed	tenacious ✓
forgiving	precise ✓	
able ✓	lovable	

How many of your good qualities overlapped into different areas of your life? Would you like to see certain qualities more present in your personal life?

Another good way to build your self-esteem is by using affirmations. Affirmations are simply positive self-statements that begin with the result in mind. They state that the situation has "already begun to change." If, for instance, you'd like to be less reactive in a certain situation, a useful affirmation might be, "I handle things calmly as they come up if I take a deep breath and think before I act."

These are the steps you take when making an affirmation:

1. See yourself making small positive steps toward reaching your goal.
2. See yourself as struggling a bit at first, but then overcoming obstacles in your path.
3. See yourself becoming someone you like more.
4. Think of self-esteem as something you already possess, but that you've just been out of touch with for a time.

Say, for instance, you'd like to lose some weight. That goal is pretty global; it's also not very measurable and therefore unlikely to be accomplished. A better way to start would be to pick a goal that is practical, definable, and attainable, such as "I'm going to lose eight pounds in the next two months." An example of an affirmation for losing that weight might go something like this:

1. Today I've really been aware of how much I've been eating.
2. I imagine sometimes I'll forget and eat too much.
3. But today I've been doing a great job at working toward my goal.
4. I used to weigh less, so I know I can do it again!

Now try this exercise.

EXERCISE
Making an Affirmation

As you read the affirmations that follow, select the ones that apply to you. Begin working with one by writing it ten times on a piece of paper. After a time, pause and wait for a response from your mind. When your mind responds, "Okay" or "True," or, "Yes that's right!" you can be pretty sure that the thought is already working for you. If your mind responds with a "No," then you know you have resistance in that area and you'll have to work a little harder on it. Write the answer your mind gives you behind the statement. Do the same process over again for each statement.

1. I am highly pleasing to myself.

2. I am highly pleasing to myself in the presence of other people.

3. I am learning to love myself more every day.

4. I am no longer dependent on another's approval for my self-esteem.

5. I now practice being kind to myself.

6. I like myself even when I'm alone.

7. I respect my unique qualities and differences.

_____

8. I am growing better every day.

_____

Now try another exercise to find out how stress-hardy you are.

EXERCISE
How Stress-Hardy Am I?

Look at the items below and score yourself from 1 to 5, with 1 meaning almost always, and 5 meaning almost never. The lower your score, the less vulnerable you are to stress.

Points

1. I organize my time very effectively. _____

2. I can talk about my feelings when I'm worried or sad. _____

3. I take the time to eat at least one balanced meal a day. _____

4. I have an adequate income. _____

5. I smoke less than half a pack of cigarettes a day. _____

6. I have at least one friend or relative I can rely on. _____

7. I get strength from my spiritual beliefs. _____

8. I regularly attend social activities. _____

9. I am an appropriate weight for my height. _____

10. I exercise regularly. _____

Points

11. I have a network of friends and acquaintances. _____

12. I am affectionate and receive affection. _____

13. I get adequate sleep and feel well rested. _____

14. I do something I really enjoy at least once a week. _____

15. I drink three or fewer caffeinated beverages a day. _____

16. I drink fewer than seven alcoholic drinks a week. _____

17. I have confidants with whom I can talk about personal matters. _____

18. I am in good health. _____

19. I take a quiet time for myself each day. _____

20. I communicate regularly with the people in my home regarding domestic issues. _____

21. I love to laugh and have a good sense of humor. _____

If your score is 30 or under, you are stress resistant. If your score is over 50, you are vulnerable and need to work to bring it down.

The Stress-Management Model

There are many strategies you can use to manage the external stressors that occur in everyday life. These are the things that don't go away—we just have to find a way to deal with them. For these there are many tried-and-true approaches, approaches you can use to deal with external stress, and most have to do with life-style choices. Eastern ideas in mental health and medicine are becoming increasingly popular.

Several ancient civilizations have gotten very positive results from these practices for a long time. Gradually, the Eastern philosophies are gaining acceptance in the United States to the point where many of them have become mainstream. The allopathic, slash-and-burn style of traditional Western medicine that treats disease as something to be removed from the body through drugs or surgery is now incorporating more of the holistic precepts of Eastern medicine with its emphasis on prevention. Interest in new therapies continues to build, especially those stressing the mind/body connection. Essentially, your vulnerability to stress can be reduced by maintaining good nutritional habits, getting lots of rest and exercise, and, generally speaking, keeping yourself maintained, body and soul.

What follows is a discussion of a few strategies you can think about using for relieving stress. In addition, there are plenty of books available on most of these topics if you want to know more about them; you'll find a list of resources to get you started in "Further Reading" at the back of this book.

Progressive Muscle Relaxation

Progressive muscle relaxation is based upon the concept that it's impossible to do two things at one time; you can't lie down and stand up, you can't be awake and asleep, and you can't be happy and sad. In progressive muscle relaxation, the relaxation response is elicited to combat the stress response. Using isometric contraction exercises, you focus on each muscle group in your body, first tensing then relaxing. Progressive relaxation works to combat stress because deep muscle relaxation reduces tension and is incompatible with anxiety. Most people can learn this technique quite easily and it's tremendously effective. There are several good tapes available for learning progressive muscle relaxation, including *Progressive Relaxation and Breathing*, for which you'll find details in "Further Reading" at the back of the book. The following exercise is a short version you can try.

EXERCISE
Progressive Muscle Relaxation

This exercise can be done either lying down or sitting in a comfortable chair. If you have a little fear of flying, you might even want to try it before takeoff!

1. While breathing smoothly and slowly through your nose, flex your feet and your toes back and tighten your shins. Hold this position for five seconds and release.

2. Next, repeat this step while tightening your calves and thighs. Hold the position and then release it and breathe.

3. Repeat the previous moves while curling your fists, biceps, and forearms. Hold the tension for five seconds and release and breathe.

4. While performing all the earlier steps in succession, tighten your abdominal and chest muscles. Hold this position and once again relax and breathe.

5. Finally, do steps 1 through 4 and tighten your buttocks as well. At this point, your whole body should be flexed. Hold this position for five more seconds and then relax and continue to breathe fluidly.

Breathing Exercises

Breathing exercises can also be useful in initiating the relaxation response and diminishing stress. Practicing breathing techniques can help change your heart rate and brain wave pattern. Deep breathing oxygenates the blood and allows wastes and toxins to be drained away. Correct breathing is central to the practice of martial arts, where it is used to aid the practitioner in centering.

There are two basic ways that we breathe and we usually use both throughout the day. In the first way, we use our chest, known as thoracic breathing. In the second way, we use our abdomen, known as diaphragmatic breathing. For stress reduction purposes, most breath techniques focus on abdominal breathing. If this sounds confusing, here's an easy way to help you identify diaphragmatic breathing.

1. Lie down on your back and make yourself as comfortable as you can. It might help you focus if you close your eyes.
2. Place your right hand on your stomach; rest your right thumb on your bellybutton. Notice that when you breathe in, your hand rises slightly. As you breathe out—your hand will fall.
3. Concentrate your attention on the continual rise and fall of your hand.

This is what abdominal breathing feels like. Trying this at bedtime might even work better than counting sheep in helping you to relax!

Breathing exercises often require a relatively fast intake of breath, which is then held for the same duration as the inhale, and finally exhaled in a relaxed and lengthy exhale.

A typical pattern is to count to four on the intake of air, hold for a count of four, and then exhale the breath to a count of six or eight. Breathing techniques can be used on their own (remember "Take 10 deep breaths"?) or in conjunction with meditation, visualization, or other relaxation techniques. Here's a short exercise to try.

EXERCISE
Abdominal Breathing

1. Lie down or sit in a comfortable position. Keep your spine straight.

2. Inhale slowly through your nose. Hold your breath.

3. Exhale slowly through your mouth. Make a whooshing sound on the exhale.

4. Continue this exercise for five to ten minutes.

Meditation

In the 1960s the Beetles introduced meditation to the general public. Again, as with the other stress-management strategies, meditation can take several forms, many of which involve clearing the mind. Here's a short version of clearing the mind for you to try.

1. Sit up straight; take a breath or two to focus yourself and to relax. Rest your hands comfortably in your lap, palms up.
2. Close your eyes and continue to breathe in and out slowly and easily. Notice any thoughts that enter your awareness. As they fleetingly appear and disappear, notice them and then let them go.
3. Continue to breathe in and out slowly and easily.

One form of meditation that is gaining in popularity doesn't require clearing your mind; in fact, it calls for just the opposite. It focuses on becoming totally immersed in the present and completely aware of the here and now. This means not worrying about the future or thinking about the past. It means noticing everything that's going on around you, what you hear and see, and how things feel, smell, and taste. This form of meditation is known as "mindfulness." Give it a try:

Select a daily activity that you do when you're alone, like brushing your hair, taking the dog for a walk, or taking a shower. Once you've selected an activity, practice mindfulness by noticing every sensation and thought that this activity evokes for you. For instance, in the shower you may notice the smell of the soap and the feeling it produces on your skin. Or you may notice the way the steam clings to the curtain or door and how wet drops of water run in little rivulets down the wall. You can listen to the patter the water makes or note the softness of the washcloth.

Visual Imagery

Another useful technique for stress management is visual imagery. Creating a visualization is like taking a mini-vacation. In a state of relaxation, you allow your mind to find a place of safety and comfort or to think about a subject that provides you with something you need. Visualizations designed for relaxation and for therapy allow people, using their imaginations, to visit havens of safety, pleasure, and beauty. They can consult with spirit guides or work on problems in their lives. Try the next exercise.

EXERCISE
Relaxation Visualization

1. Imagine being in a private and safe place. Take a minute to take note of the details of the place. Do you feel warmth? Do you smell any aromas? What do your hear? What is the light like in the place you are thinking of? Imagine being completely at peace there with everything you need.

2. Imagine there is a supernatural guide in this place for your help and protection. Visualize what your guide looks like. Is it someone you know? Is it a person, a spirit, or an animal?

3. Imagine your stress issue is an actual object with a shape, color, weight, sound, and smell. Examine it.

4. Imagine your guide teaches you how to change the stress object in some magical way that makes it a gift that can be used for good.

5. Think of the object changing its shape, color, weight, sound, and smell and becoming more benign.

6. Imagine returning to the here and now with new insights about your life.

Here's another visualization exercise.

EXERCISE
Directed Imagery

This visualization involves directed imagery and has three parts:

1. *Visualizing and feeling compassion for someone who has hurt you.*
Sit or lie in a comfortable position and take a few deep, relaxing breaths. Monitor your body for tension areas. As you notice them, relax your muscles and breathe more slowly and steadily and accept whatever images come to you.

Next, imagine that you are in a small quiet room with a chair in front of you and in that chair someone sits and waits for you. Imagine a person who has hurt you is sitting in that chair. Notice all the details about the person. How big or small is the person who hurt you; how old or young? What type of clothing is the person wearing? What does the person smell like? Is the person disheveled, angry, drunk, drugged, or frightening? What is the person wearing? What is the person's posture like? Is the person physically or emotionally threatening? Say to the person:

You are a human being like me. You are trying to survive. When you hurt me, you were trying to survive. You did your best, I guess, given your limitations and understanding of the situation at the time. I may not like it. In fact I was hurt by it, but I'm trying to understand why you did it. I may never be able to understand it. Nonetheless, I want to forgive you. I may never approve of what you did, but I can try to wipe the slate clean of the past. I can let go of my revenge and resentment. Our differences are in the past; I am in control of the present. I can leave my anger behind.

2. *Visualizing and feeling compassion for someone you have hurt.*

Next, imagine the person in the chair is someone that you have hurt or someone from whom you'd like to have understanding or acceptance. Once again see all the details of the person's appearance. Is the person big or small? Is the person old or young? What type of clothing is the person wearing? Is the clothing disheveled? Is the person under the influence of drugs or alcohol? Is the person's posture defensive or aggressive? Make the visualization as real as you can. Imagine that the person is gazing at you very calmly. Say to the person:

I am a human being, worthy, but imperfect. I am like you; we are both just trying to survive and get our needs met. When I hurt you, I was doing what seemed to be the best thing I could do at the time. If I had the awareness then of the situation that I do now, I believe I might have chosen to do things quite differently. I understand I hurt you badly, but that was not my goal. Please accept the fact that I can't do anything to change it. I cannot change the past. Please forgive me. Can we please wipe the slate clean and agree to start our relationship in fresh ways?

As you look at the person that you hurt, imagine that you see the person slowly smile, and know then that you are accepted and forgiven.

3. *Visualizing and feeling compassion for yourself.*

For the final part of this visualization, imagine yourself sitting in the chair. As before, see the details of the situation. Flesh it out and make it as real as possible. Take note of what you are wearing—perhaps you'll notice that you are dressed as you are now! Imagine what the image of yourself is saying to you:

I am a worthy human being. I'm worthwhile just because I exist and am trying to survive and grow. I take myself seriously. I, correctly, take myself into consideration first in all the aspects of my life. I have legitimate needs and desires. I can choose what I legitimately need without having to justify my choices to anyone. I make my choices, but I also take responsibility for them. I try to do my best. But because I'm human, I do make mistakes. When I make a mistake, I do my best to learn from it. I am imperfect and try to forgive myself for my mistakes. I am aware that others are equally as worthy as I am and equally as imperfect. I have compassion for them because they, like I, struggle to stay alive and get their needs met.

Imagine that the figure in the chair—you—gets up and comes over to where you are sitting. Imagine that the figure merges with you to make one whole, complete person. Relax and rest and be at peace with yourself. Breathe and float. When you are ready, open your eyes and get up slowly, refreshed, and relaxed, with a sense of acceptance toward yourself and others.

Sometimes it's useful to use this visualization if you're working on an issue with someone who has already passed away.

Self-Hypnosis

Self-hypnosis is another stress reduction technique. Actually, practitioners generally believe that all hypnosis is self-hypnosis—all that hooey about "You are in my power" is just that, hooey. You're the conductor and it's your train. You are in an altered state, yes, but you are never out of control. In fact, when you are hypnotized, you are intensely self-aware. It is an extremely pleasant experience.

Here's an example of a self-hypnosis induction you can record for yourself. Try it when you want to focus on finding a solution to a problem.

EXERCISE
Self-Hypnosis

I'll close my eyes and begin to relax,

Though at first I may be more aware of some things than I was before—

The sounds of the room I'm in, the hum of the heater, the ticking of the clock [adjust to fit your circumstances]

The sounds of my voice,

Sensations in my hands and feet,

Thoughts and certain images that float into my thoughts automatically without care.

With my eyes closed, it becomes easier and easier,

To become more and more aware of a variety of little things that I otherwise might have overlooked or ignored as I traveled through my busy day:

Feelings,

Thoughts,

Sensations.

And now I allow my awareness to become altered and my mind begins to explore and experience a little relaxation and letting go of cares and hassles.

Letting go of even the effort it takes to be reminded of where my feet are exactly positioned or my hands hang or how my fingers are held. I let go of the effort to be aware of which leg feels heavier or more relaxed as well.

It may seem that it's just too much effort to be bothered with just now.

But it will take a little time to experience the letting go.

But in my own time and in my own way, even more than before,

I will begin to drift and become even more relaxed.

I'll let go and my mind will flow down

Toward a simple peaceful place
Where there is comfort and safety—
A place where I will remain comfortably aware of what I need to
be aware of,
Not worrying, just observing.
This is a place that directs me downward into complete relax-
ation and peace.
The meaning of my words may almost not seem worth the effort
of deciphering.
It's so much easier
To simply relax
And wait,
And allow events to occur almost by themselves.
A drifting down and a settling,
And a drifting back into time and then upward toward wakefulness.
And that's fine, too;
It all belongs to me.
I have a conscious mind and an unconscious mind.
My mind will continue to hear and understand what is important
for me to know.
In my own time and in my own way
I will learn.
My experience will be altered.
I will receive what I need.
My unconscious mind will explore and guide my awareness as I
explore my abilities and capacities.

Here is another self-hypnosis induction to tape for yourself for when you are feeling uptight, anxious, or angry.

I know sometimes I scare myself
Because my mind is always active never quiet,

And because my body reacts
Sometimes I think of scary things,
But I also know there are other things I can think about
To calm myself down.
There are things I can think about that are comfortable and
   calming.
I can look at events with a new perspective instead.
I can replace those old, scary, provocative thoughts.
My mind can learn to relax.
My unconscious mind already knows all it needs to know.
It can distract me from thinking about bad or hurtful things.
My unconscious mind can provide me with relaxing thoughts.
I believe I will be happy and enjoy being unconcerned.
I will be unable to remember what worried me or
What upset me and made me so mad.
So, from now on when I enter a situation that angers or frightens me,
I can enter it knowing I am protected.
And I can tell that part of me that reacts badly
Or in a frightened, angry way
Really doesn't have to be that way anymore.
I can find other solutions or other games to play.
I can remind myself instead of the good things that could happen,
Or the fun things that could come from the situation,
Because those thoughts and fears and reactions aren't very useful
   anymore.
So, now I can relax and forget about all the fears and mistakes,
And get on with business,
Perhaps surprised to discover
That now I might be thinking about something else entirely,
And at some point, I'll know that I'll never have to feel the hurt
   and anger.
And that it's over and done with

Much more quickly than I ever expected it to be.
I can do it now and I can do it later.
I can do it whenever I wish.
I can frighten myself with old, angry thoughts,
Or I can simply relax and enjoy calming ones.
I can practice and I can choose.
It all belongs to me.
I have all the power I need.

Bodywork

Bodywork is based on the premise that the connection between mind and body is central to a healthy, well-integrated, and whole individual. Bodywork is gaining in credibility to the extent that many insurance companies now cover bodywork therapies such as massage therapy and acupuncture. Physical therapists have for years been aware of the benefits of acupressure. The aim of bodywork is to improve the functioning of all the body's systems.

In contrast to what chiropractors do, most bodywork practitioners use methods that access the body's soft tissues—the muscles and fascia. Some practitioners and their clients find that manipulation of certain areas of the palms of the hands and soles of the feet (a practice called reflexology) can be effective in minimizing headaches and all sorts of other ailments. Biofeedback, a process by which a machine measures and monitors changes in the body brought about by concentration, has been proven to be useful in reducing the pain associated with migraine headaches. Currently researchers are exploring other uses for it as well.

Massage is probably the great-granddaddy of all bodywork. Massage has been used not only by massage professionals, but also by medical people, midwives, physical trainers, shamans, and teachers of dance and martial arts. It can be a very effective aid in helping you deal with stress. During massage, activity of the sympathetic nervous system is diminished. That's the part of your nervous system that mobilizes your body for arousal. (Remember the alarm stage in the general adaptation syndrome?) Through massage, the activity of your parasympathetic nervous system is increased, your heart and respiration rates slow down, and blood flows back to your organs and digestive system. Massage can elicit your relaxation response. There are several different types of massage you can choose from including Swedish massage, sports massage, Russian massage, shiatsu, Thai massage, Chinese massage, and lomilomi (the Hawaiian variation, which loosely translated means "to break into little pieces with the fingers!").

Yoga, a cross between meditation and bodywork, is another Eastern practice gaining in popularity in this country that can be helpful in reducing your stress and thus your anger level. The origins of this art form are lost in time, but there's evidence that people in India were practicing yoga as early as 3000 B.C.E. It's a system of physical, spiritual, emotional, and mental personal development. The poses in yoga, called asanas, help to release muscular tension. When you practice yoga, you'll not only reduce your stress levels, you'll get other dividends. The asanas also stretch and tone muscles, lubricate joints, and increase circulation to internal organs. There are several types of yoga styles for you to explore, ranging from simple to strenuous. Here are a few:

- **Ashtaga yoga.** Commonly known as power yoga, this is a vigorous and fast-paced method.

- **Bikram yoga.** This method focuses on twenty-six poses and two breathing techniques for stretching and toning the body.
- **Kundalini yoga.** This method focuses on elevating kundalini energy ("kundalini" means coiled like a snake) and on meditation.
- **Istha yoga.** This method concentrates on opening energy channels through visualizations and guided meditation.
- **Integral yoga.** This method focuses more on meditative work than on physical work, although it does use certain asanas; it emphasizes selfless service, prayer, chanting, and self-inquiry.

A growing interest in herbs has people on the lookout for how natural remedies can enhance their health and well-being. Even aromatherapy, based on the idea that smell can trigger changes in health and mood, is gaining respect. Proponents of aromatherapy believe that the essential oils of plants, which are use in the practice of aromatherapy, can do amazing things. They believe that aromatherapy fosters change and healing on several different levels. At the first level, aromatherapy is said to act on a medicinal level due to the chemical composition of the oils and their astringent, stimulant, or calming properties. The next level is the more subtle action on a homeopathic level, where diseases are treated with minute doses of herbs that produce symptoms very similar to those of the diseases being treated. The last level is the use of essential oils to act on the mind. Practitioners believe that fragrance can enhance the psychic and mental state of the individual and suppress emotional problems. As it turns out, the limbic system, which serves as the brain's pleasure center among other things, is quite sensitive to odors. This might be the mechanism through which aromatherapy may effect changes. Generally speaking, pleasant odors like perfume have uplifting effects.

This is a condensed discussion of bodywork therapies. There are many more potential stress-reducing therapies out there. Not everybody agrees on the efficacy of these therapies, but if one works for you . . . why not use it?

9

Communication
and Anger

In order to live successfully among people, we all have to use some method of communication. When we think of communicating in our everyday relationships, the first thing we think of is talking. For our species, verbal communication is certainly a major part of our existence. But some people are more skilled in this type of message delivery than others. How many times have you ever heard someone say, "Oh he just has the 'gift' of gab!" or "She has a great line of B.S.!" or some such thing. These notions seem to connote that an almost mystical hand has doled out these verbal abilities. True, some of us may be more naturally able to get our messages across in a pleasant or seductive way, but everyone's ability to communicate can always be improved.

Most of the couples and families I see in practice say they feel they are unable to communicate effectively. "It's just impossible to communicate!" they say. "We try, we really do, but we are always having misunderstandings if not outright fights." Mothers and fathers say their kids don't listen; kids say their parents don't care or don't understand. Men talk about how they believe they're doing what their wives ask, but that, somehow, what they do is never good enough. Women say they feel their husbands discount them or don't understand them.

The Art of Listening

If we accept the premise that much of what is troubling to us has to do with our inability to get our perceived needs met, *then learning how to communicate in more effective ways is without doubt another critically important tool for overcoming anger.* A good way to start improving communication is to think about what communication is and how it can help us or hurt us. Communication is frequently thought of as the transmission of information, but one dictionary definition says that communication involves not only the transmission, but also the *interchange,* of information. Thus, talking *and* listening are both crucial for good communication. There may be some satisfaction in stating our thoughts, but unless someone can receive the message and validate it, we don't get much for our efforts. A classic philosophy question asks, "If a tree falls in the forest and there's no one there to hear it fall, did it make a sound?" Similarly, if we send a message and no one receives it, have we really communicated at all?

In order to meet our needs, we must continually add to the number of satisfactory interactions we have. Why? Because when our needs are taken care of and we sense we have some ability to run our lives satisfactorily, we can then develop a sense of "okay-ness." Our growing sense of safety and order tells us we will be able to meet challenges as they come up, and we can relax a bit. The more effectively we communicate, the more confident we are that we can manage our anger and other emotions. As we stay non-defensive and open to incoming messages in order to comprehend their meanings, we are less likely to react in negative ways. Provided with appropriate feedback, we

179

have a better chance at choosing the correct behavioral response for the situation.

When doing therapy with couples, I like to use an exercise that demonstrates the value of this type of feedback loop. First, each person is instructed to buy a package of his or her favorite cookies and then to entrust them to the other partner. Next, the pair is instructed that they will receive one of their favorite cookies when they do something that pleases the other person. Finally, either partner can request the return of a cookie when something displeases him or her, *but the displeased partner has to explain what caused his or her displeasure.* By using this nonthreatening approach, in making a game of it, each person's behavior becomes objectified and instantly reinforced or discouraged. Communication can blossom.

Garble, Garble

Look out for distortion in communications. This business of interactive communication is an involved process. There are so many places in the loop where the message can get messed up because a message has to pass back and forth through all types of filters before it is complete. Age, race, culture, geography, and socioeconomics are just a few variables that can play a part in garbling the intended communication. That's not even taking into account a person's belief system and personal reality.

Ambiguity in communication results when we use our intuition to interpret things, because we're actually guessing the meaning based on our own experiences and expectations about events and people. Observing families in action is a good way to experience this kind of distorted communication. Even families that appear quite homogenous report confusion. Here's an example.

Take a fairly average family by today's standards. Say Mom and Dad are recently married and Mom, really Stepmom, is a lot younger than Dad. Say Mom is one race and Dad is another. Add a teenager, who is pierced in a couple of places and into "Goth" dress and music. Pretend the teenager is almost as old as Mom. What if Mom brings to the marriage a baby from a former marriage? Let's have Dad come from the Bronx and let's have him be Catholic. We can make Mom a Protestant who came from a little village in Germany. Pretend Dad has done really well as an IT rep but never finished college and Mom is finishing her master's degree.

Now, if you believe it's possible that all these people think alike and come from the same place when they try to communicate, forget about it. It's inevitable that fragments of their personal worlds will color all their attempts at communication and collide, sometimes unmercifully, with the perceptions of other family members. How easily will communications be distorted and perhaps perceived negatively? Every family member has his or her own frame of reference and value system. Even if everyone in the family *loves* one another, understanding each other could be virtually impossible. And this doesn't even take Grandma and Grandpa into account!

Essentially, then, to begin the communication process, a message must first be put together, or "encoded." Next, it must be sent, either verbally or nonverbally, or through a combination of both. After a message is received, it has to be figured out, or "decoded," by the recipient of the message. Information about how the message was received or

181

not received must then be acknowledged somehow by a return message of some type.

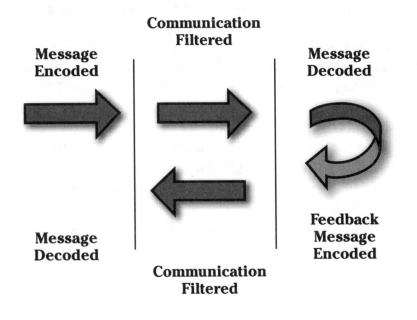

Communication Filter

Our selective perception acts as a filter through which each part of every communication must pass back and forth. It's likely there will be some type of perceptual distortion through which all our attempts to be understood must pass. No wonder this is so tricky!

The Story of Bruce and Sally

Here's a little story for you to mull over. It's an example of how distortion operates. Read it; then ask somebody else to read it and compare notes.

Once upon a time there were two people, Bruce, who was exceedingly handsome, and Sally, who was absolutely gorgeous. They had known one another a very long time, but they had, unfortunately, very little opportunity to get together because they lived on two separate islands. Although the islands did not lay at a great distance from each other, they were separated by turbulent, dark, shark-infested waters.

Several people from these islands had tried to swim the distance, but were duly consumed by the carnivorous fish. Nonetheless, one day Sally was feeling very lonely, indeed, and decided she would go to the other island to see her Bruce once more because she loved him dearly. She made her way through the dandelions, down the grassy slope by her cottage. She approached the brine-drenched docks and looked for a way to make passage. She was looking for a sea captain whom she knew of and eventually spied him and approached. Sally asked if he would be able to take her to the other island; she told him that money for the passage would be no problem. The captain took one look at Sally and told her he didn't want her money. He came up with another form of payment, though.

Mortified and offended, Sally told him to forget it and stomped off to her little house. Later though, depressed and feeling a bit desperate, she decided she would accede to his plan. The young woman returned to the sea captain and told him she would spend the night with him if only he'd take her to her beloved Bruce. The captain clapped his hands and told her she had a deal. Sally followed through on her decision, spending the night with him. The next day he kept his part of the bargain and delivered her to the other island.

183

Sally wasted no time. She left the quay and went directly to Bruce's house. The beautiful girl knocked on Bruce's door. When he opened it and saw Sally, he smiled broadly. Before anyone could say or do anything else, Sally told him what she had done to get to the island. Bruce's face became ashen with shock, and he told Sally he didn't want anything to do with her. In tears, she turned from his look of disgust and fled down his front steps, running down the lane.

Suddenly she came upon Walter, Bruce's best friend. (Walter was very rich, but not as handsome as Bruce.) Sally was crying so hard, she almost ran into him. He caught her in his arms and asked her what was the trouble? In her shame, she told him what she had done and told him Bruce's reaction. Walter smiled ruefully, then told her somewhat shyly that it didn't matter to him what she had done and that moreover he had always had great affection for her. In fact, he asked her on the spot if she would marry him. Sally considered for a moment and decided that, yes, she would.

They then went down to the harbor, where Walter carried Sally ever so gently onto the deck of his ninety-five-foot sailboat and off they sailed on the evening tide of a star-dappled twilight.

The End

So now that you've read the story, rate the characters. Rate them from most admirable to most reprehensible. Use your own standards for the ratings based on your own understanding of what those words signify. Then, find a couple of other people to do the same thing, rating each character according to their own belief systems and ethical codes. See if you all agree, and try to find out why your ideas differ from the ideas of others.

I've used this little exercise in groups, and it's very interesting to see how different individuals frame the morals and vicissitudes of the characters. There are several debates that come up that are worth considering:

- Is Sally a whore or simply a pragmatist? Is she just doing the best she can do, or is she a victim, due to her sex?
- Is Bruce admirable or a big prude?
- How did you perceive the captain? Is he an opportunist of the worst sort or a shrewd businessman?
- Is Walter just an innocent "good guy" or a predator?

Where do you stand on these issues? What are your opinions about the story? Remember, much of your interpretation is in your perception. Did the story ever directly state that Bruce was as fond of Sally as she was of him? While many people seem to think so, it is never stated directly. What was his responsibility in the whole thing? Did Sally actually have sex with the captain, or did they just pass the evening playing a lively game of dungeons and dragons? The answer could be anything—it just depends on what you read into the story, after all.

Think of the perceptions and assumptions you made about the story. Then consider what kinds of assumptions you make about everything you encounter. Good listening skills can help reduce the influence of your perceptual distortions.

Nonverbal Communication

Certain types of communication have a greater impact

than others. Nonverbal communication plays a greater role in how we interpret a message than verbal communication. Originally, researchers thought that about 70 percent of the message was contained in nonverbal communication, but that number has risen to a shocking 90 percent. Not only does nonverbal communication turn out to be more believable, at some basic level it just *feels* more dependable.

If someone tells you that she feels happy as can be, but at the same time is sobbing, tears running in rivulets down her face, it's pretty much a slam dunk that you're going to believe she's lying to you at best or pretty bizarre at worst. You will, at the very least, find this contaminated message confusing. If you're like most people, though, you're going to go with your gut and decide this person is really pretty miserable. The tears will win.

In order for you to become a more effective communicator, you'll need to keep in mind that what you're communicating must have congruence. That is, the message and the delivery must coincide and express the same thing. The nonverbal aspect of your communication can show up in many different forms, from the body language you express, to how you use your eyes, to the facial expressions you exhibit, and other forms of nonverbal expressions.

Body Language

The study of the body's posture and movement can help you determine a person's level of openness, dominance, relaxation, and self-esteem. I have a great example of how body language can be telling. A few years ago, I attended a conference on child sexual abuse where one of the presenters was an investigator for the police force. It was his job to interrogate and bust child molesters, and he demonstrated one of his techniques. He would have the alleged predator, most always a man, take a seat. Once he was seated, this cop would also take a seat, close to the perp, close enough, in fact, to make sure one of his knees was in a direct line with the suspect's "vulnerable" area. The investigator never suggested he would do damage, but he certainly suggested it nonetheless.

The detective's positioning clearly is an example of body language that fairly screamed dominance and intimidation. And according to this police officer, this little maneuver invariably worked like a charm. Although this is a rather gross, overt example, we are constantly influenced by subtle forms of covert, and in this case not so covert, communication. It occurs in all our interactions with others. Consciously or unconsciously, we unabashedly utilize our bodies for communication. In fact, one of the hardest things for us to do is talk without using some form of gesticulation. Try it sometime.

It's almost as though we're innately aware we need it to provide credibility and sincerity. The proof of this can be tested when we watch people on car phones. Even with no tangible visual audience to see them (but the occasional terrified driver going by), we can catch them attempting to use their shoulders or the hand that is supposed to be on the steering wheel, emoting like crazy, emphasizing points they are trying to get across to their unseeing listeners.

Eyes

Perhaps an even more powerfully potent form of communicating nonverbally is our use of facial expression. Foremost in terms of expressive abilities are our eyes. "The eyes have it," the saying goes, and it certainly appears to be true. We see examples of this tenet in many of our expressions. The flirtatious couple makes eye contact. The mother-in-law withers the son-in-law with a glance. When a husband gets "the look" from his wife, he knows she means business, although he may not be sure about what. Even animals are not immune to our expressions.

The eyes have been called "the mirrors to the soul." Through the eyes we feel we can get a glimpse of the truth of the matter. Our language credits our eyes with the power of deep understanding. Being able to see a thing is to equate it with being able to understand it, to clearly comprehend it. So maybe it's no wonder we pay so much attention to eyes. They can belie even heroic attempts at neutrality.

Learning how to keep your eyes from showing how you feel can be tough if not next to impossible. Cops have forever claimed they can tell if a person is lying just by watching his eyes. Are some eyes just naturally "shifty," you think? The field of neurolinguistics makes much of eyes. Neurolinguistics has even provided credibility to the anecdotal evidence that cops claim. Students of neurolinguistics say they can read the way people process information and search for thoughts in their memory simply by studying the fashion in which peoples' eyes move (with other corroborating body language).

The amount of eye contact we employ is important to our effectiveness as communicators. Too much can feel threatening, and too little can imply disinterest, which can turn people off. In our culture, maintaining eye contact about 70 percent of the time is usually considered to be adequate and comfortable. But eye contact between the sexes is another thing. I've asked a lot of men about this, and most have told me that women who make eye contact by gazing steadily at them, ignoring the 70 percent rule, appear to be suggesting a more than casual relationship or, in other circumstances, come across as aggressive.

No doubt, on some level we are all aware of each other's facial expressions, eyes in particular, but becoming more consciously aware can help us gauge the truth behind the offhand remark, and can help us move toward deeper communication and clearer understanding.

Other Nonverbal Language

Next to the eyes in importance are the rest of our facial expressions. Although some of them may be learned from the expressions of our early caregivers, some are innate and universal. Deep emotions—fear, disgust, happiness, surprise, and anger—tend to evoke similar facial expressions in people around the world.

Although your face is the most expressive part of your body, tone of voice plays an important role, too. It's not necessarily the words we listen to as much as the tone and the cadence in which they are delivered. For example, as a teenager, I remember my mother telling me to watch my "attitude." I'd say "Yes, ma'am," or some such and she'd go ballistic over the *way* I said it. I didn't get it. I'd said "Yes, *ma'am*," hadn't I? It was only when I had my own teen that I finally understood. The problem wasn't what was said, it was indeed the *way* it was said.

Body movements and gestures make up yet another form of nonverbal communication. Little kids tend to develop the bearing of their parents. One child may walk as if she is always balancing a book on her head; another may walk bowlegged like his cowboy father.

Some physical gestures are passed down from one generation to another. It's no wonder a kid might pick up a dis-
tinctive laugh or other mannerism from a parent.

Certain gestures are specific to a group of people, while
others are generalized. Some gestures, like pointing, are
rather universal and can serve as regulators. It's easy to
communicate in the bakery that you want that muffin or
this bagel simply by pointing it out. Pointing can work
equally well in places where your language abilities don't
quite measure up, say for instance in French bakeries, to
designate you want this croissant or that beignet. You can
even get it across that you want more than one of something. I'll have trois éclairs, please.

But fingers are funny things. Some hand signs that may
mean one thing in one language can mean quite different
things in another culture. (I had this pointed out to me by a
South American man who said that the supportive, "hook
'em" hand sign, commonly seen at Dallas Cowboys games,
was a no-no where he came from.) Under certain circumstances, pointing and other hand gestures can be considered quite rude. It's all in the context.

We can't take our appendages for granted when we
think about body language. Hands and arms can indicate
defensiveness, openness, indifference, and resistance. Feet
and legs may be indicative of traits, too. Movement may
suggest emotions like anger, boredom, and frustration.
Posture and breathing also contribute to the picture. Erect or
leaning posture may indicate openness or interest. Posture
that is retreating can mean defensiveness or lack of interest.
Here's a little trick about posture. Someone can be put more
at ease when you mirror his position. It sends the message
that you're with him, that you get what he's experiencing.

For example, if somebody is in a hunched position, it helps for you to hunch a bit, too. If her legs are crossed, you cross yours. If she has her chin propped on a hand, you prop, too. Hey, try it.

Breathing can also indicate emotional status. Rapid breathing may suggest the person is experiencing an intense emotion such as joy, anxiety, or anger. In contrast, deep breathing can prepare you for action or calm you and give you resolve.

When searching for meaning in communication, we are, at least subconsciously, aware of the whole package. Go for the goal of learning to be more consciously aware. It can provide material for inquiry and further clarification and ultimately help to get what you need without a lot of anger and frustration.

Proxemics

The study of physical proximity in human (and animal) populations is known as proxemics. How we use space is another way we communicate. Think about what you are saying by the way you use space. How far away do you stand from people; do you hug? Do you enjoy being hugged? How you arrange your personal furniture and how you respond to what you may consider territorial invasions are all important statements about you. Do you sit behind a desk when you meet with people or do you like to pull chairs together for a chat? All of us operate in four proximity zones with limits defined by ourselves and the culture we live in. The proximity zones are intimate distance, personal distance, social distance, and public distance.

Intimate Distance

The closest zone is known as intimate distance. It ranges from actually touching another person to standing around eight inches apart. Little kids are always hanging around in this zone; either you're carrying them or they're hopping onto your lap or sticking soggy crackers into your mouth or pulling on you. Little kids haven't yet incorporated the concept of boundaries, but adults seem to understand that and don't mind or consider kids' behavior invasive. The other group that uses this zone a lot is lovers, no surprise. This close proximity is perfectly acceptable and fine in these situations.

Personal Distance

Next comes personal distance. This is the space around you from about one and a half to two and a half feet. This is a comfortable zone for most people. You can still easily reach out and touch someone if you want to, but you are almost literally keeping people at arm's distance at the same time. At this distance there is no need to risk touch. It's the spacing we use when having a conversation that doesn't have to be too private.

Social Distance

Social distance is comprised of the area approximately four to seven feet away from you. This is the distance most people in this culture utilize when they're dealing with clients, service people, teachers, and the like.

Public Distance

Public distance ranges from around seven feet on. Celebrities use this type of spacing. The person is present, but is in no way accessible. It's the distance we keep from strangers.

You probably can see the implications and imperatives these built-in needs for territory set up. The way we choose to use space can be a very powerful communication tool. Cultures vary in their zone requirements, but they do exist in one form or another for everyone. Your space is your space—nobody wants his or her space violated. Yes, you will willingly, even gladly touch your lover and your children, but no, you do not want the cashier at the Walgreens sitting in your lap.

Why is it that when dealing with another species, we would, without doubt, be smart enough to honor what we have learned to be *their* spatial prerogatives, when within our own species we can be so dense? A coiled rattlesnake is not asking to be cuddled, after all, but a wagging-tailed dog flopped on its back is begging to be tickled. We do know the difference. So why is it that sometimes, when a situation is angry or volatile, some people disregard their adversary's territorial needs and opt for more confrontation by blithely invading that person's space? I've had clients tell me that even when they are trying to take a "time-out," their partner will literally grab them by the arm or the leg to try and force them to continue the argument. Remembering to respect another's requirements for protective space can go a long way in deescalating frightening situations.

EXERCISE
Where Is My Comfort Zone and Why?

Here's a little exercise to try with a friend or anybody who is willing.

1. Just stand where you are and ask the other person to approach you until it no longer feels comfortable for him.

2. Compare notes.

3. Did the person stop approaching while you were still feeling comfortable? Did the person get into what you consider to be your space?

4. Try the same thing with the person approaching you from behind or from the side. Did the person feel comfortable approaching you more closely from these positions?

5. Ask yourself what accounts for your comfort or discomfort. Did you know the other person well? Was the person of the opposite sex or from another culture? Was the person very much older, more powerful, or younger than you? Would it have made a difference?

6. Compare notes again.

Examining your beliefs about territorial prerogatives and becoming aware of what makes up who you are as an individual can make all the difference in how you feel about what's happening to you. If you came from a family of stoic individuals and you married into a family of hug-crazed folks, there will be differences to explore. Messages become more confusing the more distinct the culture, but this is not to suggest one way is right and the other wrong. It is only to point out that some of the most well-intended gestures can cause other people to feel uncomfortable and annoyed or even threatened and angry. And the threatening person didn't even know that he or she was doing it.

Lend Me Your Ear

A great way to help you calm yourself when communication seems to be shutting down or heating up is to truly try to hear the other person. A useful method for doing this is known as active listening. When you think about it, "to listen" sounds rather passive, but active listening requires more of you than just sitting there on your lily pad. You actually think about what's being said, provide feedback, and encourage the other person to clarify what he's saying.

There are several good reasons why it might behoove you to use this technique. Active listening helps out when emotions are aroused, when you're angry, and when perceptual distortions are on overload. It can also be used to clarify confusing or unclear messages. When the flow of dialog is moving quickly and lots of things are going on, active listening can help you remember important issues surrounding the communication. It also demonstrates to the other person that you are truly involved and paying attention to her.

Active listening is a process that entails five important actions:

1. You observe and physically orient yourself to the person speaking. Doing something else at the same

time—changing the baby, shooting hoops, or fiddling with the remote—are verboten.

2. You acknowledge the speaker and provide feedback on what you see and hear.

3. You provide encouragement for the speaker, which aids in continuing the communication.

4. You ask the speaker for clarification of information, when needed.

5. You are responsible for an interpretation of the communication or its meaning.

There are several techniques that you can use to improve your active listening skills, but make sure you use them appropriately, because you could end up sounding bored or even mocking—neither of which is your intent.

One-Word Encouragements

On a basic level, probably the simplest and yet most easily goofed-up technique in active listening is the monosyllable. Sitcoms featuring shrinks always feature this tact. For example: Someone in the sitcom (in this case the patient) says something. The listener (in this case the doctor) says, "um" or "huh" or "oh?" It's just a little thing, not enough to break the speaker's train of thought, but it's enough to encourage more disclosure and keep the momentum going. A slight nod of your head works nicely, too, but take care not to go overboard.

Paraphrasing

Paraphrasing is another method of active listening that can work well, but it, too, has its drawbacks. Basically, somebody makes a statement and you repeat what you heard—only in your own words. Doing this correctly does require some practice, though, and if you're too literal, you can come off as a little demented or learning impaired.

For instance, your son says to you, "School sucks. Nobody even asked if I felt like going to the river during spring break. What a waste." How do you interpret this? It sounds like there may be two ideas contained in this statement. As a parent, you may want to soothe your kid or you may feel like he should hang tough. Either way, you might come across as discounting. What's a parent to do?

As a fledgling paraphraser, you might try, "I hear you saying that during the break the guys are going away, but they didn't ask you to go." Your teen is probably going to assume, since you're his parent and the relationship is tenuous at best, that: (1) you're rubbing it in his face or (2) you're having an awfully hard time processing such simple information. But hang in there; there are good reasons for trying this technique. In stating in your own words what you believe your teen is saying, you help yourself to avoid misinterpretation. And you stay busy trying to determine what your teen means rather than getting defensive and blocking the lines of communication.

A better tact might be asking a question like, "You're saying everybody else is going but you?" This leaves out the assumption that your teen wasn't asked—maybe there's some other reason. Because we are human and like to be right, much of our time is engaged in weighing and balancing what other people say. We are constantly evaluating their "rightness" or "wrongness," determining how they measure up.

We also spend too much time rehearsing how we're going to respond and, in the process, we don't hear much of what is actually being said. Paraphrasing is one of several tools that keeps us from doing this, thus allowing for a more open flow of information.

Rather than making a statement about what was said, it's better to paraphrase what's being said and give it back in the form of a question. Why? Because, through the use of questions, the road is open for further explanation. The message, after all, may be a dual one. Is the problem with the friends or the school? You don't really know. By asking clarifying questions, you get more of the picture. The focus becomes refined and generalities can be avoided. The event can then be understood within the context of the other person's feelings.

Even if your interpretation is wrong, who cares? In fact, it's actually better, if it allows for the other party to add more information. That leads to an improved and more finely honed exchange. You might get a follow-up message that lets you know it really doesn't matter so much about the trip; that's just part of it. The real problem is the biology test that was a disappointing wipe. Now you know what's *really going on* and you can decide to respond more effectively.

Reflective Listening

Reflective listening operates on a still deeper level. This type of response includes some of your thoughts or feelings about what the person has told you. As long as you keep your thoughts and feelings respectful, reflective listening can be used when the other person is having difficulty discussing an issue. By providing this type of feedback to the speaker, you promote a supportive environment and enable him or her to have an understanding of how the communication has affected you.

Simply pay attention to the emotional part of what the person is saying. Then as you become a better and better listener, you'll ask yourself what the person is saying, doing, thinking, and feeling. Depending on whether you decide the emotion is what's important or the content of what the person is saying is more important, you can construct a reflection. Why do it? Because it helps the *other* person to become aware of his or her own feelings, which can be either good or bad. (Remember, it doesn't really matter what the emotion is; it's how you handle it that counts.) It aids the speaker in exploring all the nuances of the feelings experienced and in accepting them for whatever they're worth.

If you can demonstrate care and understanding for the other person, you may be adding to the safety of what might otherwise be an unpleasant or volatile situation. When people feel safe to explore what's truly going on, they are better able to master their negative emotional side without reacting in negative, unproductive ways. Also, through reflective listening, you show you are trying to understand how the other person is experiencing the world. Empathy is very nurturing and comforting. It helps build intimacy and provides the promise of more satisfying future interactions. Most of all, it can really deescalate a potentially dangerous situation.

Here's a little formula you can start off with, if you like, for practice purposes: When making a reflective listening statement, be sure to use an appropriate, objective introductory phrase followed by a clear description of what you observe. Be sure to take your nonverbal communication into account, as well.

Make sure you *own* your observation, meaning you

should acknowledge that what you're saying doesn't need to be taken as a law. Owning the statement shows that you know it's *your* idea, thought, or opinion, and it's based upon *your* personal perspective. Here's an example of a reflective listening statement: "Hey, there's something I'm trying to figure out. When I see you pacing back and forth across the room like that, I'm wondering if the loss of that project really has you confused?" Remember, the goal is not to be *right;* the goal is to be interested and on the same wavelength. When a person disagrees with you, it's no biggie, because this allows the person to clarify his or her feelings by supplying you with enlightenment, something more accurate that aids communication.

When using a reflective listening statement, do just that, reflect. Share your impressions and feelings and be done with it. Resist the temptation to end your musings with, "If I were you . . ." because this type of proselytizing can backfire! The person may not be seeking a solution for the problem, especially from you, and offering one may, in fact, be a total turnoff, especially if your interpretation of what's going on is inaccurate. So try not to give advice, tempted though you might be.

Empathic Listening

If you can provide help by using empathic listening, so much the better. Remember, everyone is just trying to survive, doing the best they can, and you need to recognize the struggle. Empathy helps you avoid making judgments

Still, because of our competitive nature, it's hard to avoid trying to make our own points. When you're not really open to the other person, when you're happily building a case to dismiss the other person and his ideas, it becomes easy for even useful information to get scrambled. In utilizing an empathic response to somebody's dilemma, you join with them. For instance, you might acknowledge that although you haven't been in the exact same situation, you remember what you felt like during a similar experience. This can be very soothing and encourage further communication.

The point is, try to hear the whole story before passing judgment.

Delivering Feedback

Try to become aware of any lack of congruence in what you are receiving from someone. If the information doesn't fit the facts of what you see going on, it's your job to point out the discrepancies by giving feedback. In providing this appropriate information, you let the speaker know how she's doing and you reinforce improved communication. Used properly, feedback can build trust within the relationship—but try and provide feedback that is nonjudgmental. We all want to be liked, to feel valued, and to feel as if we belong, so being judged as wrong, different, or inferior brings up defenses that we tend to turn into feelings of anger in order to empower ourselves, which doesn't aid honest communication. That's why becoming a good listener plays an important part in managing anger. By remaining neutral in your feedback—descriptive rather than evaluative—you reduce the chances of getting a defensive reaction.

In giving feedback, go for specificity rather than generalities. When things get too general, they become incomprehensible. By addressing specific, limited behavior over which the receiver of your feedback has some control, you help provide for positive outcomes for yourself and the speaker. Being specific will help you both get what you need from the exchange.

Global requests with no way to measure them are usually doomed to failure. Laments like, "Why can't you just get your act together and shape up?" or "I wish you'd be a better husband!" are bound to be ineffective in making any positive changes. With global laments like these, your teenager is not sure if you're suggesting she should go into acting or become a weight lifter. Your husband hasn't a clue why he's so hateful and doesn't know what in the world he can do to please you.

Use feedback sparingly at first until you've learned how it goes over. Feedback should be something that is solicited rather than imposed. Learn to limit the amount of commentary you provide to the amount the receiver can handle at the time. Too much feedback can come across like constant interruptions and may seem aggressive. Giving feedback is not supposed to be mistaken for nagging. After all, there is such a thing as too much of a good thing. Feedback should be used as a corrective mechanism for individuals who want it and are willing to learn how well their current behavior matches their proposed intentions.

Group therapy is one useful tool used by psychotherapists that utilizes the feedback of people within the therapy group to effect beneficial change in the group's members. Group theory takes into account the individual's personality, which is illustrated in the Johari Window. The window stands for the persona, or a person's personality structure, which is divided into four panes.

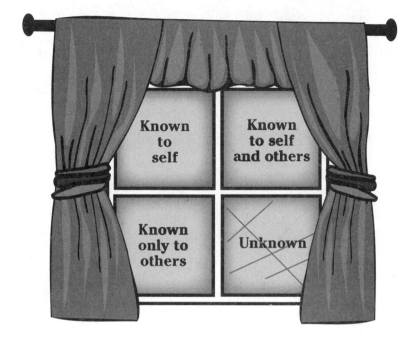

The Johari Window

The upper left pane holds things that are known only to yourself. These are things from the past or present that are considered secret for one reason or another, generally things considered to be nobody's business but your own (that you pick your nose when you're alone, for instance). It is sometimes also referred to as the hidden agenda area.

In the upper right pane, are things known to yourself and to others. These are things you have chosen to share or that others have found out. An example in this pane might be that you love Italian food and hate karaoke. This is the pane of honesty and openness. It represents a person's contact with reality.

In the lower left pane are found things known only to

others. These include how you come across to others—are you dumb or smart, does your nose hair need clipping, do you have egg on your blouse, and other such observations by others. This area is also known as the blind area.

Lastly, in the bottom right pane are things about your personality that are unknown. It's full of unknown behaviors and motivations that neither you nor the others with whom you interact are aware of. Perhaps these things could be accessed in dreams or by hypnotism, or maybe not, but in any case, for now, this pane is irrelevant.

The group therapy process works with the lower left pane, which contains things known to others, but not to you. It is through the power of feedback that group therapy helps many people experience phenomenal change. Even outside such a therapeutic structure, feedback in your daily life from those around you can promote positive change in you and in others.

Three Blind Men and the Elephant

In order to get a truly clear picture of a situation and to communicate with accuracy, it's essential that we try and obtain as much information about it as we possibly can. Because knowledge is critical to understanding, we need to remain open to data and not allow our personal prejudices to cloud our perceptions. Otherwise, we operate at a disadvantage like the blind men in the old story. There are several versions of this parable, here's mine:

Once upon a time there were three blind men living in a far-off place in a time long ago. It was a very exotic place, and there were many unusual creatures that dwelt there.

One of these unusual creatures happened to come into their village. The creature was an elephant—something no one had ever heard of at the time. The three blind guys went to investigate.

The first man approached the kindly elephant (it's a "kindly" elephant, otherwise the story could get pretty brutal). He reached out his arm and felt the elephant's side. He ran his narrow palm up and down the creature's brawny, warm, mud-caked flank. Satisfied that he knew all there was to know, he stepped back and smiled.

The second of the trio approached the colossus next. Tentatively he touched a leathery ear that danced with flies and shivered to and fro. He chuckled as he gleaned the implications. He returned to the village.

The third man must have lost his bearings for he approached from the rear (fortunately upwind at the time). The happily placid pachyderm stood still while the third man testily pulled on the animal's hairy tail. Convinced of his vision of the beast, the third blind man retreated.

That evening the three discussed what they knew of the beast, all of them sure of their interpretation. The first to make his view known was the man who held the tail. "The elephant is like a large snake," he attested. "You always were too fond of your wine, good sir," said the man who had touched the elephant's broad side. "Surely you must be raving if you think the creature is a snake. For no, the elephant is more like a house made of mud baked in the sun, large and hard and high." "You're both lost to Buddha, you fools," said the one who stroked the ear. "The elephant is like a sailing boat that runs to the wind," he declared.

The shouting and recriminations didn't stop until the village constable arrived. They never learned the true nature

205

of the elephant, because each insisted his view was the correct one and would not listen to the others.

Self-Disclosure and Intimacy

We are all a little bit like the blind men. We're conditioned by our beliefs and personal limitations. It may not be easy to let go of our prejudices, but it's essential we do if we want to get a true picture of what is really going on. The more knowledge that we have about a situation, the better. The golden rule of communication should be: clarify, inquire, and clarify some more, and use all the tools available to help understand what is going on. One such tool is self-disclosure.

Providing feedback is one form of it because it lets other people know what you're thinking and why. But true self-disclosure goes even further—it puts you "out there." It allows others to know you better by providing information on feelings you are experiencing now, feelings you've experienced in the past, and your thoughts about yourself and about others. When you self-disclose, you're sharing information about your needs, desires, and expectations in the past and in the present. Self-disclosure contributes to improved relationships in several ways.

It's been found that, generally speaking, people who self-disclose are better liked than those who do not. The reason is, in providing information about ourselves, we give power to others. That is to say, the more we share about ourselves, the easier we are to read and to understand by those around us. In light of the new information others receive, what we do becomes more predictable, makes more sense in context, and becomes more acceptable. When people are able to put our behavior into a conceptual framework and come up with a rationale for what we are doing, they can relax. We are seen as less threatening and elusive. We seem "safer." As we become safe, others get less defensive. Our relationships are then free to deepen and become more relaxed and satisfying.

There are several other rewards for using appropriate self-disclosure. One is that, in engaging in it, we gain increased self-knowledge. In putting out more information about ourselves, we encourage more feedback. We learn about the impressions we make on others and in doing so have an opportunity for rumination. It's a reality check that works well.

Have you ever heard someone say, "Do you hear yourself talking? Do you hear what you're saying?" Getting this from someone you trust can surely act as a useful wake-up call to check in with yourself and what you're thinking. As self-knowledge increases, it demands further clarification that allows you to more clearly define your own needs and the needs of those around you. This type of self-communication helps reduce anger and build intimacy because knowledge of yourself and others is critical to forming truly close relationships. Willingness to disclose builds the synergy needed for deepening a relationship. Disclosure breeds disclosure. The more available you become to others, the more encouraged they are to respond. Self-disclosure becomes kind of an "I'll show you mine if you show me yours" sort of thing.

Also, in disclosing what you have done or felt, you may experience a reduced feeling of guilt or regret. The Catholic sacrament of confession is, after all, based on the notion of disclosure, and it's said to be good for the soul. Going to therapy works on the same kind of principle. Being able to talk about your perceived failures and disappointments with a trusted, careful confidant can go a long way toward restoring your sense of feeling good about yourself. You no longer have to keep the bad thing or mistake hidden, and you're still alive and, hopefully, still valued. Once it's out in the open and you've faced it, the power of the "bad thing" evaporates. You may also find that self-disclosure energizes you. It's tough keeping important things about yourself hidden—good things and bad. Spending all that time and effort on not being yourself lessens your ability to enjoy what's really going on around you.

But, people can also overdisclose and this can lead to problems. Therein lies the rub. You've probably known people whom I call "glompers." These people just meet you and suddenly you're their bestest buddy. Glompers call you constantly, they like to give you presents for no reason, and they appear at your door at odd hours. They want to tell you right away all about themselves. They assume that you really do want to know all about their sexual habits, their bathroom habits, everything. What these people aren't getting is that disclosure, like most other things, is best done in moderation. Glompers can push anger buttons. Because they don't respect your boundaries, they make incorrect assumptions that can feel very threatening.

Good relationships simply require balanced self-disclosure. Sometimes, while I'm doing therapy with newly married couples, one of the partners reports that the wife (or husband) is using dirt from the past, shoveling big time, trying to win a point when fighting. It usually turns out that one member of the dyad has told the other something very intimate and risky before building a trusting relationship.

The relationship hasn't reached a level where such loaded information is really safe. They didn't achieve balance yet, so the "ammo" was all on one side.

As an example of how the levels of disclosure build, say I'm beginning with you. Perhaps I tell you something fairly innocuous like, "I really like Mexican food." Okay, all well and good. This information is not going to cause worlds to collide. Now, if you respond to me that you and beans don't get along so well (a little risk here) and you prefer Chinese food, we have disclosed appropriately and our relationship might just deepen a little bit. Say next I tell you that I used to ditch classes in high school and you tell me that you did the same thing. We're still balanced; we're moving right along. Consider that we have several more of these types of exchanges, all the while revealing things that are heading into more intimate territory.

In a regular relationship, based upon a person's personality style, these disclosures will take some time to come out as you stick your toes into the surf deciding the safety of the tide. Now pretend we're to the point where I tell you that I smoked pot (and may have even inhaled) and you respond by telling me that last month you knocked over a bank and, moreover, you killed the bank guard. I will probably want to head for the hills. The loop of disclosure has broken down. The scale has become unbalanced. This is not to suggest that if you are an armed robber you should look only for others of your ilk, but merely to point out how disclosure is good only in so far that it serves to deepen and enhance a relationship. Disclosure is not meant for shock value or for exculpation.

On a more realistic front, the value of disclosure comes up in the therapy setting when one partner has been

209

agonizing over whether or not to tell the other about an affair. Notwithstanding the health issues that need to be addressed, the question always comes back to, what purpose will it serve? Is your need to disclose actually a need to confess, a need for absolution? Who will this information help or hurt? How will it improve the relationship?

When disclosing information, take a tiny second to weigh what you are trying to achieve. In order to avoid an angry confrontation when the topic is heavy or heated, planning in advance can help you get what you need. That goes not only for thinking about what to disclose, but how to prepare the message, as well. In a dicey situation where somebody is getting angry, it can help lower the volatility level if you can get information across in a way that is non-threatening and makes sense to the person with whom you're interacting.

Sending the Right Message

Messages can be divided into three categories: whole messages, partial messages, and contaminated messages. Normally, the goal for everyone is to produce whole messages that can be understood from top to bottom. I'll tell you about those in a minute, but first a few words about the others.

Partial Messages

Partial messages, a kind of shorthand, sometimes work, too, but they are more likely to be misunderstood, especially by someone who's not in tune with such an abbreviated form of communicating. Partial messages can be used effectively by some parents and their children, business partners, teams of various sorts, and couples who've been married forever. It isn't mind reading; it's more like being of "like mind." Experts at sending and receiving partial messages have the same frame of reference. They usually have a bunch of experience in watching the other person operate. Because they're on the same wavelength, very little is necessary to get a message across. When it works, it's great because it's easy. Partial communication reinforces itself not only because it is easy, but also because it's intimate, similar to a secret language you share with somebody. Time and distance seem to have little effect on those who can successfully operate with this style.

Here's an example of a partial communication that works. Say a couple has just spent the day cleaning the garage. They've made good progress with the exception of a collection of athletic shoes in a pile by the door. The husband might say something like, "We've got to figure out how to organize this mess." The wife agrees. Time goes by and the smelly pile remains. A couple of months later, they're in Home Depot walking down an aisle and spy a metal shelving system designed for holding things. "Like that?" the wife says. He says, "Exactly," and they get the shelf. (Now they have a pile and a shelf.)

Contaminated Messages

Contaminated messages are incongruent messages that just don't make sense. They may take a couple of forms. One type of contamination occurs when the verbal communication doesn't match the nonverbal message you receive. For instance, if your boyfriend, clenching his jaw, screams at you, "I'm not upset," you're quite likely to be dumbfounded over the inconsistency between the decibel level of his assertion and what it is he's saying.

Another form of contamination comes from communications that seem to convey two different things at the same time. For instance your wife tells you she doesn't want to cook dinner, but doesn't want to go out, either. These types of messages can be very confusing.

Whole Messages

Why should whole messages be the aim of most serious exchanges, and what makes them superior? Well, they provide lots of information about *why* the message is coming to the listener. They provide the softening effect of what is known as an "I" statement. This is the cornerstone of assertive communication that is discussed in the next chapter. These complete transmissions include some reflection of feelings and needs on the part of the person making the communication. They are considered less confrontational than other types of communication and allow the receiver some freedom in how he or she will respond. Most important, perhaps, is that *comprehensive messages are exceedingly useful in conflict situations and situations that appear to be escalating out of control.*

How do they work? Whole messages provide a sweet setup for understanding. They give the receiver of the information some background information on where the idea is coming from in the first place by reporting on what most would agree are objective, reliable observations. The sender of the message states exactly what he or she is observing or experiencing without any added speculation, inferences, or conclusions. It's the facts, ma'am, just the facts.

For instance, you say, "I see you're shivering." This is not debatable, at least in this universe. Either the person is shivering or the person is not. At this juncture you don't question the source or nature of the shivering. Then you report any thoughts, musings, or conclusions you may have about the nature of the observation you just made. For example, "I'm thinking you must be cold," or "I'm wondering if you're feeling sick," or "You didn't eat that gross old chorizo, did you?" At this point you are free to add an addendum to what you're thinking that may include value judgments and attempts at synthesizing. For instance, "You know, they say undercooked sausage can have all sorts of bacteria on it."

The next step may be a bit harder because it includes information on your feelings. Hearing about feelings, good or bad ones, may feel threatening to the person on the receiving end. Under some circumstances, hearing people express even positive feelings for us can be embarrassing or make us uncomfortable. Certainly, facing someone's anger and other negative emotions is frightening because it threatens the listener's self-esteem and may feel physically threatening as well. But as long as there is truly no threat, anger and other emotions are important to express because emotions are the building blocks of intimacy. In our sausage example, a statement about feeling could be something as simple as, "I'm really worried about you and I'm angry that you could be so careless." At least you're sending a message that you care.

The last part of the whole message can include a statement about what you need or would like to have. Nobody knows what you want better than you do. When other people know what pleases you or frightens you, they may gain greater empathy and understanding. They are better able to modify their behavior to meet your needs. When emotions can be expressed and exchanged safely, we are gifted with a clearer comprehension of who we are and how we interact with each other. This is not a time to be judgmental or pejorative. It's simply a chance for you to let your listener know what would please you.

So, your whole message would be, *"I see you're shivering. You didn't eat that gross old chorizo, did you? You know they say undercooked sausage can have all sorts of bacteria on it. I'm really worried about you and I'm angry that you could be so careless. I want you to call the doctor."* It's a silly message, but it does include all the elements needed. It provides observations, thoughts, feelings and desires. The listener is now free to choose how to respond. It's a heck of a lot better than hearing, "What dumb thing did you do, you jerk? Look at you. You better call the doctor." After all, it may not have been the sausage at all.

EXERCISE
Practicing "I" Statements

Here are four scenarios. Read each one, think about what you would say, and then write down the "I" statements you believe work the best in each situation.

Your wife knows you're short on funds this month. Nonetheless, when you go to the closet, you discover she's apparently bought out the mall. You feel as if she's disregarding the fact money's tight or maybe rubbing your nose in it. You would like her to take some of the stuff back.

1. Your description of the situation:

   I _____

2. Your thoughts regarding the situation:

   I _____

3. Your feelings regarding the situation:

   I _____

4. Your needs regarding the situation:

   I _____

You're supposed to meet a friend for lunch. You planned to meet at 12:00 and your friend knows you have a packed schedule. The restaurant won't seat you alone and so you wait. At 12:30 your pal strolls in. Your stomach is growling, but at this point you don't have time to eat.

1. Your description of the situation:

   I _____

2. Your thoughts regarding the situation:

   I _____

3. Your feelings regarding the situation:

   I _____

4. Your needs regarding the situation:

   I _____

You asked your boss for the day off so you could take care of some medical problems. He says fine, and you schedule your medical procedure. The afternoon before your test, your boss comes into your office and says sorry, but no day off. He needs you for an important client in the morning.

1. Your description of the situation:
   |

2. Your thoughts regarding the situation:
   |

3. Your feelings regarding the situation:
   |

4. Your needs regarding the situation:
   |

Your husband has your car and you're late for work. You try his cell phone to let him know you need the car, but he doesn't answer. You're worried you may miss an important meeting. Finally he returns.

1. Your description of the situation:
   |

2. Your thoughts regarding the situation:
   |

3. Your feelings regarding the situation:
   |

4. Your needs regarding the situation:
   |

Certainly, the idea that we can always create whole messages and be conscious at all times of the types of disclosures we're making and how they affect those around us is a best-case scenario. It implies that the world is an orderly place where everybody is playing by the rules. The soldiers sleep at night and march only in the daytime, that sort of thing. The real world doesn't operate like that, obviously. These techniques are just ideas that some people have found useful. Still, if we can be actors in our own dramas and know our lines even some of the time, we'll be angry less of the time, and our stories will have more happy endings.

In the old West, gunfighters who could shoot well from the hip were considered awesome. It's tough to do. Usually, taking aim and being prepared is better. And like shooting or any other skill for that matter, the more you practice, the better you get. These communication concepts and tools may seem stagy and fake when you first try them, but as you become used to them, they become second nature. The more they work—and they do—the more normal they seem. Like the caveman with his magic rituals, you can gradually incorporate these methods of communicating into your typical patterns. When your exchanges become more pleasant (and you find yourself getting what you want and being less uptight in the process), your skills simply self-reinforce.

Choosing the Right Moment

When you're aware of where you're coming from, you can be a better judge of what really is going on. If you are tired, disappointed, or angry, you're probably not in the best frame of mind to go toe to toe with Rick Jr., who snuck out last night. If you're feeling ill or unappreciated, it's probably not a good time to get into it with Mary, who left the car with an empty tank.

You should also be aware of other people's condition and the condition of the environment if you want to get your message across. Evaluating what's going on with other people can help you predict the type of reception your message is likely to receive. Making sure your surroundings are appropriate ones for discussion of issues is a good idea, too. Trying to solve problems in bars, at sports events, in front of friends and relatives, or in the middle of the night is usually counterproductive. Timing is everything, as they say.

There are always going to be circumstances that require immediate attention or even confrontation. Spontaneous situations will always require fast action, but hopefully they will not be frequent. One "good" thing about chronic problems is that they're going to happen again, so, unless they're life threatening, you don't need to discuss them while they're occurring, and most likely that wouldn't be productive anyway. For example, if John has just come home tanked again, rest assured you can wait to talk about it when he's coherent. If drinking is a problem, it's probably not just a one-time thing, and finding a solution is not going to magically happen. Trying to deal with problems like this in the heat of the moment can elicit some major reactions in the other person, so it's better to talk about the problem when the emotions of both parties are in control.

Blocks That Don't Build

If all this technique stuff makes it seem as though you have to be a wimp in your conversations, don't worry. There will always be a place for assertive confrontation. The more you are aware of and understand what others are doing when they try to get their thoughts across, the better served you will be. Most of the time you can get what you need without becoming angry or steamrolling other people.

But it's difficult to be perfect, so it is normal for all of us to unconsciously sabotage a lot of our efforts to communicate with one another. Even supposing that we come from the same background and share the same set of references, it's easy to make some blunders. We may even have the best of intentions, but we all tend to fall prey to certain things that block our ability to listen and interfere with good communication.

The Need to Compete

One of those blocks in communication is our urge to compete—it's part of being human and it's built in. There is only so much to go around, and, according to Darwin's notion of survival of the fittest, we are all stuck with needing to stay on top of things. Because we are self-conscious, we tend to like to look at others and thereby gauge how we're doing. Frequently, when others are trying to communicate with us, we get hung up on not listening to them so much as comparing what they're saying or doing to some preconceived measurement system that is uniquely our own. This may not even be a conscious thing, but it occurs, and we end up wondering: Does what he's communicating go along with my vision of reality? Is what they're telling me a threat? Am I smarter, prettier, or more clever than she is? On a basic level, competition is appropriate, because we are simply trying to stay alive. Nonetheless, this type of competitive inquiry can be disadvantageous when trying to accomplish clear communication.

A Dozen Blocks to Communication

There are several bad habits that can block communication, but as we become aware of them, we can let them go and improve our chances of getting a clearer message across. Here are twelve bad habits to avoid:

1. Filtering a message through your own belief system can cause you to misunderstand the meaning. Be aware of that tendency—we are all at its mercy.
2. Using clichés can tend to sound phony or insincere.
3. Responding defensively may distance the speaker.
4. Giving advice can turn off the other person by making him or her feel inferior or incompetent to handle things.
5. Operating with an inaccurate understanding can be frustrating to the other person.
6. Pretending to understand can make the other person feel the situation is hopeless and he can't get his accurate message across.
7. Ignoring the communication or changing the subject can cause the other person to feel rejected, devalued, or uninteresting
8. Using long-winded communication may distance the other person due to boredom.
9. Playing psychologist causes intellectualization and distances the other person.
10. Being judgmental and evaluating distances the other person and generates defensiveness.
11. Patronizing is condescending and can make the other person feel inferior.
12. Mind reading can limit the possibilities for truly understanding other person.

Rehearsing

Many people who come from dysfunctional families use a block known as rehearsing. As children, many kids who come from an environment that was unsafe or unpredictable developed this way of thinking about things as a tool for survival.

Say in your family, Mama was depressed a lot of the time. Say sometimes she'd get crazy happy, too. You never knew what it was that made her so sad. You could never predict when she'd be in one of her up moods, either. All you knew was that when Mama was sad, she'd cry and act funny and sometimes she'd lock you in the closet and scream at you that she wished she never had you. Sometimes, your mother would hit your back with a ruler or a light cord. When she'd get happy, Mama would smoke a lot of cigarettes and sing songs or maybe she'd just leave for a couple of days and you'd be alone until you called Aunt Sally to come and take you to her house.

By rehearsing, you could have a plan A and a plan B. When you saw "sad" signs, you'd stay outside or hide the ruler. When you saw cigarettes come out, you'd keep Aunt Sally's phone number close by. Under the circumstances these are great, adaptive strategies. But as an adult, if you "front load" circumstances with preconceived patterns, your actions could be counterproductive and you could risk losing some potentially wonderful possibilities.

The Need to Be Right

As human beings we love to be right. It feels good. It also blocks communication. Sometimes things just aren't that important. When our self-esteem is high, when we're in a good place, trivia just doesn't matter. It's usually the people who feel out of control who have the greatest need to control and be right. If this need is great in your relationships, take a look at what's going on. This holds true for everyone, lovers, business associates, parents, and children. We have to choose our battles.

If you ask yourself who is really running the show, you might be surprised. You stand a better chance of having your message openly received if you can remember to be clear, direct, and supportive when composing a communication. If you can remember to stay in the present and address yourself to your concerns in the here and now, you stand a better chance of being heard.

Although it takes two to tango in a relationship, learning good communication skills increases your chances of keeping your listener involved. Communicating clearly helps you to feel as though you've been heard and helps you to get your needs met in a safe way.

10

It's Down to You: Assertiveness

The world, it would seem, is full of paradoxes. The more we know about the universe and everything in it, the more mysterious it appears to be. From Newton to Einstein, from Einstein's special theory of relativity to the discoveries of the Hubble telescope, our ideas of what constitutes reality have both imploded and exploded. Is life what you make it, or is it all preordained? Do we have control or, as the philosopher Leibniz wondered, are we just dreamers in a dream? Whatever we believe, since we are here for the time being, we are required to interact with others. Depending on your approach, those interactions can be a source of considerable pain or profound pleasure.

Developing an ability to be more assertive is a very positive step in overcoming anger and making life more rewarding. Assertiveness training can help reduce stress and anger by teaching you how to stand up for your legitimate rights without bullying others or letting them bully you.

Take care, however, not to confuse being assertive with being aggressive. Having a working definition is a good way to start understanding what it means to be assertive. The dictionary says that "to assert" means "to make a statement confidently without the need for proof or regard to evidence." It says that assertiveness training is a method of training someone to act in a bold, self-confident manner. Note that there's nothing in either definition that suggests that assertive people try to enforce their beliefs on others or lord it over them in any way.

If you accept that we are all responsible for our actions, then becoming more assertive makes good sense. If much of how we perceive the world is based upon what we believe, it just follows that becoming more assertive gives us more options. In fact, research has demonstrated that use of assertive techniques is beneficial in combating anger and in lifting depression and interpersonal anxiety. It's a key element in working with family violence.

The Early Years

In the late 1940s, a researcher by the name of Andrew Salter started to look at what was dubbed "assertion." He described it as a personality trait. As you remember, the personality is considered to be a rather unchangeable structure. It was believed, therefore, that assertion was a yes-or-no proposition. It was felt that like other personality traits—extraversion or neatness, for example—you were either born assertive or you weren't.

Later, in the 1960s, other researchers began to look at this personality style. Two psychologists, Lazarus and Wolpe, redefined assertiveness as the ability to express rights and feelings. In their research, they found that everyone had some ability to be assertive, and that some people might behave assertively in certain situations even if they appeared to be totally ineffectual in others. For these two social scientists, then, the goal was to increase the

225

number and variety of situations in which folks could be assertive. In doing so, they figured they could reduce the situations where people either became passive and collapsed or went ballistic and blew up.

The 1970s brought more ideas on the subject. Self-esteem (and all its implications for self-efficacy and happiness) came to be a hot topic. Researchers like Alberti, Emmons, and Jakubowski explored how assertiveness fit in with the self-esteem issue. They determined that less assertive people simply didn't feel very worthy or equal to other people. This breed couldn't even seem to find legitimate grounds to object when others mistreated them—they didn't feel they were entitled to be treated fairly. The researchers postulated that self-esteem might be tied into early parental messages. You can easily surmise what a depressing state of affairs that would lead to in a person with such low self-esteem. What a great breeding ground for resentment, pent-up anger, and potential violence!

Styles of Interpersonal Behavior

Your ability to be assertive in any situation ties into many of the messages that you, as a child, received about your value. If you were nurtured and felt as though you were a worthy person as a little kid, you were lucky and you probably grew up with a pretty good sense of mastery. You probably developed a belief system that assured you that could handle yourself in most situations.

If you were unlucky enough to have grown up in a household where you didn't receive messages of worth, your self-esteem was not nurtured. But now, as an adult, you can work on that little deficiency with good results.

Getting to know how you operate is the first step in enhancing your assertive abilities. In the course of our daily lives, most of us tend to use several behavioral styles, depending on what's comfortable for us in a specific situation. We may vacillate, but most of us use a fallback position when our back is to the wall, so to speak. It is the one we use in a knee-jerk way when things are feeling out of control or threatening, when we're reactive rather than proactive. Once you're more aware of the kind of situations that really get to you, you may want to think about replacing your traditional anger style with a less hostile or passive one.

There are three basic styles of interpersonal behavior—aggressive, passive, and assertive—plus one hybrid, the passive-aggressive style. I'll explain how these four styles can all operate in our lives, but first try the following exercise to see if you can figure out what your preferred interpersonal style may be. Remember, we all mix our styles, but you might find one that is dominant.

EXERCISE
Finding My Interpersonal Behavior Style

Each of the following statements describes a situation and a response. Try to put yourself into each situation, and decide if the response applies to you. If it does, place a check mark next to that statement.

○ A person on the road moves into a position in front of you very slowly, forcing you to slow down. You pull around in front of him and cut him off.

⊘ You are arguing with someone who pushes you, and you push back.

○ You are in a job interview and you become tongue-tied when you try to enumerate your strengths.

⊘ In a small group, you can easily state your opinion and are willing to discuss it with those who disagree with you.

○ You are delayed in getting home because you stayed in a restaurant chatting with a friend. When you arrive home and your spouse is angry, you tell your spouse it's none of his or her business.

○ After waiting in a restaurant for twenty minutes for the menu to come, you loudly express your annoyance to the waiter and leave.

○ Because the sales lady won't leave you alone, you agree to buy a dress you don't really want.

⊘ You feel as if you're doing all the work on a team project at work. You tell the group, "I'd like to see if we couldn't divide the project tasks a bit differently."

⊘ You'd like to get a raise, so you make an appointment with your boss to discuss it.

○ Your parents are coming to town and they want to stay with you. Your apartment is very small and you'd rather they didn't, but you acquiesce and tell them they can stay at your place anyway.

⊘ A repairman overcharges you. You explain the problem and ask that your bill be adjusted to correct the right price.

⊘ You're in a movie theater and the person next to you keeps talking throughout the movie. You whisper to him that you can't hear the movie over his chatter.

○ You are in a group discussion of current events and, although you disagree with the person speaking, you keep quiet for fear that you'll be criticized for your opinion.

○ You are talking to your spouse and he or she doesn't appear to be listening. You stomp out of the room.

○ You are meeting a friend who never arrives at the destination. At your first opportunity you call the friend and demand an explanation.

○ You are set to speak in front of a group. You are nervous, your voice breaks, and you feel the need to leave the room.

○ Twenty minutes before a date, your friend calls and cancels. You are disappointed and say so.

○ A neighbor has his TV turned up very loud. You call the police.

⊘ When you see a person you'd like to get to know, you are able to introduce yourself easily.

○ Your brother wants to use you car because his is in the shop. You have an appointment, but you cancel it and let him use the car.

○ You are waiting for a parking space. A car pulls out and you begin to pull in, but another car pulls in front of you and takes the spot. You drive on and find another place to park. Then you come back to the pushy person's car and key the side of it.

○ A person cuts in front of you in line at the market. You sarcastically say, "S'cuse me?"

○ You are feeling happy and confident. Your spouse is grouchy. You tell your spouse you're sick of all his or her bad moods.

⊘ While being driven to an appointment by your partner, you get a speeding ticket. You tell your partner how dumb it was to be driving so fast.

As you read the characteristics of the different interpersonal behavior styles that follow, take a look at your answers to the previous exercise and see if any patterns emerge. Then you'll have a good idea of where you're coming from and what you may need to work on in order to operate in new and more productive ways.

The Aggressive Style

If you operate primarily with an aggressive style, these are things you might recognize in yourself:

- You are frequently involved in fights.
- You feel that people continually accuse you of things.
- You find it difficult to get along with others.
- You often feel as though people are trying to push you around.
- You feel the need to dominate in the workplace or at home.
- You tend to express yourself through yelling or violence.

The verbal components of an aggressive style include:

- You violate other people's rights by expressing feelings, thoughts, and beliefs in a way that is dishonest, threatening, sarcastic, condescending, or inappropriate.
- You give the other person "you don't count" messages.
- You express your anger in an out-of-control or hostile way that usually results in your feeling ashamed or wrong.
- Your aggression tends to break effective communication.
- Your aggression aims at winning through the use of domination, power, and control.

Nonverbal components of the aggressive style include:

• Your use of finger pointing, fist shaking, or other offensive postures.
• Your eye contact takes on the form of a stare down.
• Your facial expressions are angry or overexaggerated.

Why do people operate in this way? Aggression, especially if it's backed by violence, is extremely effective for gaining compliance. After all, when fighting wars, we don't send in the social workers; we send in the Marines! Some people resort to aggression when the threat facing them is just too great to handle in any other way. An aggressive response occurs almost spontaneously when people find themselves in acutely dangerous situations where quick, decisive action could preserve their safety. It's the "fight" part of the flight-or-fight response: Kill or be killed. Other people use this technique when they feel superior to others and believe others have no personal rights of their own. People may act aggressively when they simply don't have the skills to behave in a more assertive way.

While these tactics may work in truly threatening situations, they are not a healthy choice for a behavioral norm. Aggressive people may not get crossed much of the time, but they are not well liked by those around them. Others see them as obnoxious and gradually find ways to avoid or ignore them. Unfortunately, the attempt of others to avoid or ignore aggressive people can "push their buttons" and in itself serve to escalate the aggressive behavior, possibly to a danger point.

The Passive Style

If your typical behavior is passive, you may be the type of person who wants to avoid conflict at any cost. Here is a list of traits you might recognize in yourself if you have passive tendencies:

- You continually placate other people.
- You feel as though you are walking on eggshells much of the time.
- You feel as if you don't deserve any better than what you have.
- When others are rude to you, you believe it's your fault.
- You silently suffer rather than stand up for yourself.
- You feel as if the world is against you.

The verbal components of a passive style include:

- You use an apologetic manner when expressing yourself.
- You send "I don't count" messages when communicating.
- You violate your own rights by neglecting to express your honest feelings, needs, thoughts, and beliefs.
- You take on the martyr role.

Nonverbal components of the passive style include:

- Your eye contact is indirect and evasive.
- Your body language conveys anxiety, helplessness, or weakness.
- Your facial expressions appear sad, sulky, helpless, or worried.
- You exhibit nervous gestures, like hand wringing, inappropriate giggling, or throat clearing.

Passive people behave the way they do in order to avoid rejection from, or the anger of, others. Passive people mistake assertiveness for aggression and want to avoid it. Passive people may believe they have no personal rights or that by not making waves they are being helpful. Or, like aggressive people, they simply may lack the ability to be assertive. They operate at the flight end of the fight-or-flight spectrum. In the short run, they survive, but they can still fall victim to anger, and when enough is enough, passive behavior can manifest in its flip side— aggression.

The Passive-Aggressive Style

In Greek mythology there is a story about a robber, albeit a charming one, by the name of Procrustes. This crook boasted about his hospitality and in particular about his special bed. He bragged that his wonderful bed could comfortably accommodate anybody, and he liked to invite people to try it out. As soon as Procrustes' unfortunate house guests took him up on his offer to enjoy the bed, they discovered how it worked. If the overnighter was too tall, the tricky thief would simply lop off the guest's head. If the guest was too short, that was no problem, either. He'd simply be put on the rack and stretched until he was the appropriate length.

Procrustes is like someone with a passive-aggressive personality style. On one level, what he does seems perfectly straightforward and compliant (amiably inviting his guests to enjoy his comfortable bed), while on another level he's truly sending aggressive or hostile vibes (by killing or torturing his guests). The passive-aggressive person acts out conflict without ever acknowledging it.

Overtly, the passive-aggressive's behavior seems okay, but underneath the covert message is definitely nasty.

If you're thinking about the snotty crack you made in a stage whisper or how you left the dog poop on your neighbor's step after you got angry, you may be recognizing a few passive-aggressive tendencies of your own. It's the style people use when they want to get their needs met but are afraid of the consequences of going about it in a straightforward way.

Here is a list of traits you might recognize if you operate with a passive-aggressive style:

- You placate others, but at the same time resent doing it.
- You use a lot of sarcasm in your interaction with others.
- You feel a need to "get even" when you don't get your needs met.
- You don't clearly communicate your needs to others.

Verbal and nonverbal components of the passive-aggressive style can be a melding of the behaviors found in both the aggressive style and the passive style.

The Assertive Style

The assertive style differs from the other three styles in several ways. Its main focus is on the self rather than on others. It is simply having the ability to express your own legitimate rights and feelings, allowing you to get what you need in an assertive fashion. The assertive style allows you to act in your own best interest without angering yourself or others. Because you are expressing yourself in a way that doesn't cause hostility and push other people's buttons, you can be nondefensive and your stress level stays low. You don't wind up feeling guilty for being out of control or aggressive and you don't wind up resenting the fact that you were a passive wimp. If you are assertive, you may recognize some of these traits within yourself:

- You feel you have the right to your own opinions, yet are respectful of others' opinions.
- You believe you have the right to say no to others and understand they have the right to say no to you.
- You believe in your own worthiness and the worthiness of others.
- You can communicate your needs clearly to others.

The verbal components of an assertive style include:

- You give "we both count" messages.
- You honestly express your beliefs, thoughts, feelings, and needs.
- You leave room for a compromise in each situation.
- You deal with situations without having to dominate them.

Nonverbal components of an assertive style include:

- You use body language that connotes confidence and strength, such as upright posture or firmly standing your ground.
- You use appropriate eye contact that does not seek to dominate.
- You speak in a fashion that is clear and expressive, using a voice that is not too soft or too loud.

- You maintain a facial expression that is congruent with what is being said.

As you discover that an assertive style works better than the other styles, you'll find that assertiveness becomes self-reinforcing. It is simply a more effective strategy for getting what you legitimately need from your environment. In responding to others, you can either choose to be oppositional or you can choose to reflect on how you are being affected by what is going on and proceed from a reevaluated perspective. Once you get into the habit, the time you need for reflection will become quite brief. It all comes down to you; being assertive is a choice that you can make. Fundamentally, the assertive style is about your self-image. Behaving assertively is not just something you do; it's who you are.

Assertiveness Techniques

Assertiveness training is based upon legitimacy. At the core of the system is the precept that you have rights regarding yourself and your life:

- You have the right to use your own judgment.
- You're not responsible for justifying your behavior.
- You are responsible for the consequences that result from your judgments and behaviors.
- You have the right to change your mind.
- You have the right to make mistakes.
- You have the right to not know everything.

Not knowing everything is tough on men who are usually taught they must be competent in all things. You probably never heard a mother tell her son, "Honey, it's okay if you're a little backward and don't do well in school. In fact, if you're not a success in life, that's no big deal, either." Not likely. Girls can usually get along being a little dense; because of society, they're not expected to be rocket scientists, and besides they can always marry someone smart.

Exercising the right to say "no" without feeling guilty is tough on women who are usually taught to believe they must appease others and be polite. So, like men with their competency issues, women have to try a little harder to refute irrational beliefs that they have to be nice to everybody.

Here are some guidelines (appropriate for both genders and any age group) for practicing saying no *for the right reasons:*

- **Say no to demands that are inappropriate, particularly to those demands that violate your own values and standards.** This is a really hard one for kids. Peer groups are powerful influences and it's hard to feel left out. The pervasive appeal of gangs in our society attests to kids' longing to be part of a group or a cause. Parents can help their kids by discussing this issue with them.
- **Say no to committing other people to something without their knowledge or agreement.** "For sure, Sally would love to baby-sit," and "No, no, Frank would be happy to have the association meeting here," are examples of this type of perverse generosity.
- **Say no to doing for other people what they should be doing for themselves.** This doesn't mean you shouldn't help somebody in need. It means only that babying people usually leads to other problems

237

down the line, causing them to become dependent. It just enables them and makes you resentful. This type of enabling system can frequently be found in families where there is substance abuse and a parent or spouse covers up or makes excuses for the abuser.

Generally speaking, say no to anything that will make you feel less than the best you can be. This is not being selfish; it's just being self-interested.

Sadly, people may try to impede your attempts at being assertive by throwing these common blocks to keep you off balance:

The "laugh off." People may try to laugh you off, responding to your calm statement as though it were a joke, trying to belittle or ignore it.

The "turn around." People may turn things around to make you the source of all their problems in their eyes. The best defense, after all, is said to be a good offense.

The "beat up." If people can't really fault your logic, they may respond to your assertion with a personal attack.

The "delay." People might counter your assertion with, "Not now, I'm too tired to think about it." Or, "Yes, yes, but let's talk about it later, okay?"

The "why?" People may block your assertions with a series of "why" questions in an attempt to throw you off track. This shift can devastate you if you're not ready for it. (But used positively in assertive communication and conflict resolution, inquiry can redirect people if they become tangential. Asking a question like, "I see that you're mad, but I don't understand why you always get like that"—is fabulous for getting somebody back to reality.)

Luckily, there are ways around these little gambits! Try out the following troubleshooting tactics and see how they work for you.

The Echo Technique

Direct the "why" right back where it came from. Shift the focus of the discussion from the "why" to an analysis of what's happening between the two of you. You can put the person blocking you back onto the issue by saying something like, "We're off the point. We're not here to talk about old issues. Let's talk about what is happening between us now."

The Broken Record Technique

Using this technique, you repeat your assertion calmly. Without getting sidetracked, make your point over and over and respond to any objections the other person might make by saying something like, "Yes, I know that you're feeling annoyed right now, but nonetheless my point is . . ."

The Assertive Inquiry Technique

When somebody personally attacks you, one way of responding is with an assertive inquiry. It's actually a prompt for criticism from the other person, but it's purpose is to gather additional information. You might say, "I understand you don't like the way I behaved last night. What is it that bothered you exactly?" Accepting or owning some of the responsibility for the problem takes the wind out of the other's sails to some extent.

The Assertive Agreement Technique

This technique is close to the assertive inquiry technique, and it's another good method for diffusing potential escalation. You simply respond to the criticism, admit you made an error, but separate the mistake you made from you as a bad person. "Wow, I did blow it and completely forgot our date. I really am usually more responsible," might be an appeasing response.

The Circuit Breaker Technique

This technique should be used cautiously because it may come across to some as discounting or condescending. In this technique, you respond to any provocation or criticism with monosyllables or very clipped statements like, "Yes," "No," or "Perhaps later." Men tend to do this naturally, but women don't usually get it—they don't understand that this may be a man's signal that he is through talking about an issue for the time being.

The Assertive Delay Technique

This technique allows you to put off a response to a challenging statement until you are calm and in control and able to deal with it appropriately. It sends a message of respect to the other person while still providing you with time for needed reflection. An example of this type of response might be, "Yeah, that's a good point. I'll have to think a little more about it. I do want to work on it. Just let me have some time."

The Whole Message Technique

Probably the most valuable tool in assertiveness training is that wonderful whole message (also known as the "I" statement). Done correctly, this communication states your assessment of the situation, the feelings the situation has produced, and the beliefs behind what has been said. In using it, you put forth a message that doesn't come across as evaluating or blaming the other person. It merely expresses your feelings. The listener learns the feelings and the reason for the feelings and is given the opportunity to respond or clarify regarding the situation. It allows the receiver not only to understand your feelings and the context, but also allows for further exploration.

"I" statements connect the feelings to behaviors. Rather than hearing, "You're inconsiderate, you made me cry," you hear something you can comprehend, such as: "I feel like crying when you leave and don't say good-bye." Blame is replaced by objective clarification, allowing for channels to remain open and for defenses to be lessened through empathy.

If you choose assertiveness as your style of communication, your assertiveness will ensure you achieve these goals:

- Equalize and balance the power of all parties.
- Compromise and negotiation in solving problems.
- Allow for the expression of a person's legitimate rights, feelings, and needs.
- Deal with those situations and people that you would rather avoid.

Here's a chance for a little assertiveness practice.

EXERCISE
Learning to Be Assertive

This exercise has three parts.

First, think of a situation where you've had trouble asserting yourself in the past or one you anticipate could be a problem for you in the future. Think about how you can improve the situation by adjusting your beliefs about it.

1. State the problem situation.

2. How are you presently behaving in the situation?

3. What beliefs support your current behavior?

4. What behaviors would be preferable in the situation. (Remember! This is your behavior, not the other person's!)

5. What beliefs would help to support your improved behavior?

Second, think about a time when somebody's behavior was a problem for you. Construct an "I" statement to deal with the situation.

1. Describe the situation as you see it.

2. State what you thought about what was going on. (Don't forget, you can use inquiry for clarification!)

_____

3. State how the situation made you feel.

_____

4. Explain what you would like to have happen in the situation (your "I" statement).

_____

Finally, take a moment to think about the people in your life you have loved or admired. What qualities did they possess that made you feel that way? Jot down any qualities you'd like to develop in yourself. Remember, you are in charge!

_____

_____

_____

_____

_____

_____

_____

_____

By practicing being assertive, you'll help your sense of self-efficacy to grow.

11

Conflict, Confrontation, and Those Nasty People

So, you've made it almost through the whole book. And maybe you have really thought about and agreed with some of the ideas regarding how to reframe your anger, better manage your stress level, communicate more effectively, and be more assertive. Perhaps you've done the exercises and come up with great new insights for yourself. That's great. Good for you!

The good news is that you do have the power to behave, within your own spheres of influence, in a fashion that promotes better relationships with the people you encounter. The bad news is, you won't always be around people who actively use the same techniques you use or are open to the same ideas as yours.

Conflict and confrontation will still occur no matter how many new and improved behaviors *you* employ. People still have different needs, and they'll still try to get those needs satisfied in the best way they can. Remember, their needs may be just as legitimate as yours, even if they are radically different. Even people with similar interests can have conflict. But, conflict can be an opportunity not only for change, but for growth as well.

What Is Conflict, Anyway?

We know that many people resist change, yet change can oust outmoded ideas and behaviors and surprise us with opportunities for growth and success. Conflict can really be constructive, because it creates a crisis, which forces change. The word "crisis" itself is a variant of a Greek word meaning opportunity, and many times it takes some sort of crisis or conflict before there can be movement. Handled well, conflict and confrontation can result in a unity of purpose between the people involved that produces better collaboration than existed before the conflict. So, the first step in dealing with conflict may be to start looking at it in a new way.

Conflict results from a perception of threat and what appears to be a win/lose situation—if you get what you want, I can't get what I want. But the way to resolve a conflict is to see it as a win/win proposition. Look at a conflict this way:

- Ask questions and clarify your assumptions regarding what the other person wants or doesn't want. Ask the person what his or her reasons are for wanting or not wanting something.
- Analyze the person's interests and issues, and analyze your own as well.
- Discuss problems before discussing solutions.
- Communicate what you want and why it is you want it. At this point you might decide it's not a conflict after all.

247

Determine whether or not the conflict represents a true threat and not what I call a faux conflict. Sometimes what appears to be conflict is not truly threatening, but rather a misunderstanding or situation that makes little difference in the scheme of things.

Next, be aware that conflicts occur because people have different interests and it's their *difference of interests* in conflict. Consider this example:

Two parents come in to my office with problems over childrearing issues. They've been bickering and name-calling over whether or not to use corporal punishment on their rambunctious school-age child. Mom says, "No, there are better ways to deal with disobedience—things like time-outs, token economies . . ." (Mom's been reading *Parents Magazine* and such.) Dad says he was switched "plenty" when he was a kid and he turned out just fine.

Is this an example of a true conflict? Is it a matter in conflict because of different interests? They were fighting about which method of discipline was best after all. True, each party thought they knew best. But at the heart of the issue was their child's welfare. There was no conflict or disagreement about that. Actually, getting the couple to see that they had their main interest in common went a long way in helping to unravel a faux conflict and resolve the problem. Both parents had the interest of their child in mind, and both were doing their best to see that their child was disciplined in a way that would lead her to become a successful adult. They just had different ways of going about it. By analyzing interests and issues and discussing problems before solutions, the couple was better able to communicate what they wanted and why. After the situation deescalated, the couple was able to strategize and find some integrative solutions to get their mutual needs met. They left the office feeling as though they were on the same team.

When interests are in conflict, resolution is a bit more difficult because there is less common ground to stand on. Each party has an objective that is independent of the other person, but solutions can be found. Remember that conflict resolution doesn't always require a fifty/fifty solution, only one that is nominally acceptable to both parties. Relationships always require a little give and take, and the goal is to find a win/win solution.

There are a few basic principles to keep in mind when attempting to resolve conflict:

- Problem solving should be regarded as a collaborative effort to resolve a mutual problem.
- Each partner should demonstrate his or her willingness to change before the partners attempt to find a solution.
- Problems should be defined and addressed before solutions.
- Problem definition should be brief, specific, and in the present.
- Only one problem at a time should be addressed.
- Solutions to problems should be modest, mutual, and realistic.
- Solutions should be detailed and clearly understood by each partner.

Maybe if you can give a little this time, next time you'll get a little more. Try to be flexible when working toward solutions, and always have a plan B in mind before entering the resolution phase.

The first thing to look at is whether or not the other person is seeking a solution or just wants somebody to listen. Try to remember this, because if someone wants to vent on an issue, it may come across as confrontation, when, in fact, the person is merely telling you about his or her frustrations. Try to figure out if that's the case before you get your hackles up and become defensive.

You may know some people who constantly vent their frustration and anger. These people may have reasons for their chronic anger—they may be ill, have family problems, or even be depressed. Sometimes people who chronically vent may not realize how destructive their constant anger can be until after they've blown their relationship. One client of mine said with a perfectly straight face, "Well of course I rag on Jim, but it is *his* decision to bleed."

Sometimes venting and problem solving can take place at the same time. That's because, after venting for a few minutes, the person may feel listened to and be better able to look at his or her issue less emotionally.

Tricks of the Trade

There are some general rules of engagement you can use if you find yourself in a situation that just can't be analyzed, compromised, or negotiated away.

Be Careful of Generalizing

Saying things like "You always" do such and such or, "You never" do blankety-blank can make things become true. Such statements can begin to shape a self-image in the other person that eventually becomes a self-fulfilling prophecy. Generalizations can make a person feel defensive because they place the other person in a hopeless, no-win situation. So be sure that you request behavior change only. Instead of telling someone to stop "doing" something, try telling that person what you would like him or her to do instead.

Stick to the Topic

When people don't stay with the subject, there is undoubtedly an underlying, unresolved, or unspoken issue. Bringing into the argument past grievances or annoying character traits is basically a dirty fighting technique known as "brown bagging." Listing old injustices just throws things off track. Dredging up old scum confuses the focus of the current problem situation and tends to escalate everything to an unsolvable, out-of-control global fight.

Stay in the Here and Now

Check in with your partner. Find out if what you're hearing is what your partner means. Here-and-now questions get here-and-now answers. Avoid questions such as, "How can you be so bullheaded [or stupid, or uncaring, or dumb]?" for which there are no answers.

Remember to Communicate!

Let's review some of the communication techniques and pitfalls we discussed in Chapter 9:

- When you mind read instead of really listening to what's going on, you lose the chance to find an acceptable solution to the dilemma. Respect your partner by taking his or her communication literally.

- Restate what you've heard, ask clarifying questions if you need to, and look for areas of agreement. Offer an apology (in whole or in part) if you need to—it won't kill you.
- Try not to cross-complain, which means responding to someone's complaints with complaints of your own. You'll never solve anything that way.
- Make sure to avoid sarcasm because it can come across as passive-aggressive—which it is.
- Try to be consistent in expressing your needs and concerns, otherwise you may confuse your partner.
- Try never to give advice unless it's requested and even then give advice in moderation.
- Try to avoid communication that is blaming or shaming. Blaming your partner just escalates defensiveness and closes down a person's desire to compromise about a situation.
- Avoid pulling rank. Reminding your partner that you're older, or smarter, or that you make more money is not going to endear you to your spouse in any way, shape, or form. Remember, problem resolution is a joint endeavor.

Don't Question the Other Person's Motivation

It's unproductive to question motives with comments like "You do that just to upset me, don't you?" If that were the case, the relationship would be pathological. Although certainly such relationships do exist, most of us would not be willing to live with anyone who purposely tries to upset us. If we stayed around, the relationship would be sado-masochistic. Assuming that this is not true of your relationship, try to utilize the paradigm that the other person is simply attempting to get what he or she needs and is not trying to hurt or injure you.

Use Assertive Techniques and "I" Statements

"I" statements show that you own the problem or concern and don't make the other person feel defensive. Demonstrate your willingness to solve the problem and hear the other person out. Acknowledge the other person's point of view, which shows that you respect the other person's right to his or her own conception or perception of the problem. (But it doesn't mean you agree.)

Don't Argue When You're Sick or Tired

Fatigue, like drugs and alcohol, inhibits thinking and increases the likelihood of an overly emotional response. Therapists won't try to work with people when they are under the influence; why would you want to? If you don't feel well, you're liable to overreact or may not be able to concentrate on the conversation. Conflicts and problems, especially chronic ones, are best handled when both parties are rested and alert.

Set a Time Limit

One hour of discussion is enough at any one time. Freud taught us that! Partners often seem to think a good cathartic session has to be an "all-nighter." Forget it. There are times when everyone needs to refuel. Exhaustion can lead to an exacerbation of feelings of isolation and defensiveness and can lead to a bigger blowup if not downright violence. Agree in advance that either party can take a "time-out" if it becomes necessary. If you need more than an hour to get things settled, agree to give it a rest for twenty-four hours and set a time to work on the issue the next day.

Choose the Right Moment

Timing is critical when it comes to conflict resolution. When you are preoccupied, tired, or in the middle of something else, it's much more difficult to feel open to negotiating for changes. Say John is cranky before 10:00 A.M., definitely not a morning person. Seven A.M. would not be the best time for Sherry to talk about issues. Remember, the "good" thing about chronic behavior is that it always comes back. So, when working on chronic issues, use your noodle, and consider the best time to talk about the problem— when both partners are in a good mood.

Some More Creative Tricks to Defuse Conflict

Here are a few more quick tips for containing conflict:

- Try using an endearment in the middle of a fight. Even when we are angry and upset it can be reassuring to know that we are still loved and cared for. We like to know that we are still someone's "honey" or "stud muffin."
- Stay within touching distance, as long as violence is not an issue in a relationship. By remaining accessible to the other person, you demonstrate your trust and connectedness.
- If you're feeling accusatory, try asking a question instead. For instance, instead of saying, "You like Mary better than me!" Try something like, "Do you feel Mary is more attractive in some ways than I am?" Questions provide for clarification of issues and are

lower on the volatility scale.
- Use a little bit of humor in tense situations. As long as it doesn't come across as sarcasm, humor can help deescalate troublesome issues.
- Try to think outside the box. Creative solutions can sometimes work wonders.

Here's an example of how a creative solution worked for two of my clients. "Mary" and "Mike" came in for help with their relationship. They were thinking about getting married in the near future, but suddenly everything about their relationship felt wrong. Mary had been in therapy before and believed in its value. Mike, on the other hand, was quite skeptical and came into the office saying so.

Mary worked in real estate and had big dreams for her future. Mike worked for a local construction company, was happy with his life as it was, and did not appear to have grand aspirations or any desires to make big changes in his life. The couple obviously had different personal goals.

When it came to the marriage ceremony, they also had different ideas. Mary's parents had offered to provide the couple with $10,000 for their wedding expenses. Mary envisioned being led down the aisle and given away by her dad. She had picked out a dress and started searching for a reception site. Mike, on the other hand, thought the whole thing was ridiculous and a big waste of money. He said he felt the money would be put to better use if it were invested. Mary protested that her parents weren't giving them the money for investment purposes, but for a wedding.

The session ended in a stalemate. They did agree to come back the following week, however. Meanwhile, I formulated some thoughts on what was going on. I surmised that perhaps Mike was feeling a little inadequate under the circumstances and a little resentful of his future in-laws and their money. As it turned out, boy, was I wrong!

When they returned the following week, Mike confided he almost didn't return for the session and it was only Mary's urging that got him to come to the office again. He said that last week's session had helped reinforce his belief that therapy was a waste of time. They started in again on the marriage issue. Mike groused that he thought the wedding should be their own private affair, conducted on the beach by a female minister who was also his friend. Mary said he was just being cheap.

Once more, a stalemate developed. Several things were suggested as solutions to the dilemma, but none appeared satisfactory. Then, almost as a joke to lighten the situation, I suggested that they have two weddings, one for Mike and a second one that would appease Mary's parents and provide Mary with the fairytale wedding she had pictured. Mike and Mary stopped in their tracks. They looked at each other and smiled. Next thing, before I knew it, Mike was up and out of his seat. He pulled me up from my chair and threw his arms around me in a great bear hug. Dancing me around the office, he thanked me for the brilliant idea!

It seemed Mike had a very deep belief that marriage was between two people, and his resistance had nothing whatsoever to do with money. The rest of the session was spent planning how it would all be arranged. First the couple would have the private ceremony and later they'd have the formal, public one. They both left the office delighted with the rather unusual solution to their problem.

Putting It All Together

There is an old toast that says, "May you live in interesting times." Well, we certainly do! The world seems to be spinning at an incredible pace, and we will continually be challenged to keep up with novel concepts and technologies. With this in mind, it's crucial that we maximize our ability to adapt to ever-changing demands on ourselves—and our environment—by using the skills we have available.

The key element to remember is, we all do the best we can with what we've got, and we are not doomed to perpetuate nonproductive behaviors. We are in charge of who we want to become. You truly do have the power to sculpt the shape your life will take! The sculptor may be ambitious. The sculptor might indeed be an artist ready to share with the world a vision of beauty. Without the right tools, though, the sculptor's true potential will never be realized.

I hope you have found in these pages a few tools you can utilize to create the life you were meant to have.

Appendix

More Exercises

W hen practicing a sport over and over again, your body develops a "muscle memory," which programs it to respond automatically in certain ways that not only make the required task easier and more natural, but also make you better at performing it!

A "practice effect" also occurs when you consistently work on deangering with the exercises found in this book. The more frequently you can become aware of the state of your physical body and the more you practice and fine-tune it with stress management techniques, the more easily you'll be able to influence your mood.

Here are a few additional exercises for you to consider.

Meditation

Why do so many people have such a difficult time appreciating their uniqueness? Sure, their uniqueness may include some imperfections, but that's part of being human. The important lesson may be that by accepting your limitations and celebrating your unique capacities, you can stop bashing your self-esteem and you can begin to forgive yourself. Forgiveness can free you to try new, less painful approaches to life.

The following meditation script is a metaphor about the value of uniqueness.

EXERCISE
Go Figure

There's not really one right way to relax or to enter into an altered state.

Maybe that's because in nature, no two things are exactly alike.

We talk about symmetry, but it's just symmetry.

When it comes to us, we think we need to do things *the right way*, perfectly.

Yet when it comes to other things, we seem to value the odd or the strange or the unusual.

Collectors' items become prized *because* they are unique.

Or maybe they're valued because something about them is a little bit wrong or imperfect.

It's said that true beauty has a certain aspect of the extraordinary.

It's never apathetically consistent.

It's also been said that "beauty is in the eye of the beholder."

Look at a garden.

The flowers that appeal to you won't necessarily appeal to me.

Every flower is unique.

Each one is just the way it should be.

Look around a museum.

On the walls hang works of art from different periods and cultures.

Artists' styles are all somewhat different, even if they are all Fauvists or Impressionists or Classicists.

They all bring something different to their work.

Maybe the proportions of some of the paintings seem odd.

It doesn't matter.

We value the unique perspective—when it's art.

Consider your clothing.

The styles you wear won't necessarily look right on me.

Sometimes things that seem all wrong can really be all right.

It's just a matter of perspective, after all.

Trying things in new ways can become exhilarating.

Exploration becomes imperative if things don't all have to be the same.

After you've explored your collection and your garden and your museum and your closet,

And after you've decided what you want to keep or give away,

You can go ahead and do it.

Mindfulness

The hectic pace of your daily life can get you running on overload and can easily contribute to making you feel as though the world is an unfair and nasty place. You can wind up feeling pretty sorry for yourself and quite annoyed about the situation. This type of thinking is sometimes extremely hard to avoid, but it can really up the amperage of your anger battery.

Here's a five-minute mindfulness exercise to try when you're feeling frazzled.

EXERCISE
Being There

On a day when the weather is pleasant, take five minutes to go outside.

Find a comfortable spot to sit. You can either use a chair, a wall, or sit on the grass—whatever is most comfortable.

Breathe naturally. If you have a watch on, check to see how much time it takes you to inhale and exhale ten times. (If you're not wearing a watch, just try to become aware of the pace of your breathing.)

Next, listen for your heartbeat. Sometimes this is not easy to do, so if you can't feel your heart beating, just find your pulse instead. You can locate the pulse point on your wrist by placing your middle and ring finger directly below your hand on your other arm on an almost direct line down from the junction of the index and middle finger of your opposite hand. Unless you're an EMT or a nurse, this method can take a little practice. If that doesn't work, don't worry—try using your index and middle finger to find the pulse point on your neck. (This method is a little more obvious, but generally easier to do.) It's located directly under your jawbone almost straight down from the outside corner of your eye.

Once you've either keyed into your heartbeat or your pulse, explore it. How strong is it? How fast is it? Does it feel as though it's regular or surging? Is it comforting to feel your blood flowing through your veins, or does becoming aware of its movement seem rather frightening? Experience what examining this intimate life force means to you.

Continue to breathe regularly. Now, explore what's going on around you. What does the quality of the light feel like to you? Is it a sunny day or is the sky filled with clouds? Can you see shadows? Do you see any dew? Is it morning, noon, afternoon, or evening? Become aware of how each time of day has a different feel to it. Do you feel invigorated or sleepy? Are you relaxed or on edge? Notice how you are affected by the time of day.

What can you hear? Is it quiet and hushed? Is there a lot of background noise? Do you hear traffic, dogs barking, or children? Can you hear sirens or birds? How do these sounds affect you?

As you continue to breathe regularly, notice how your body is feeling. Notice the temperature and the feel of the clothes you're wearing. Do they feel heavy or restrictive or itchy? Do they feel light and loose and comfortable?

As in the story of Goldilocks and the three bears, do your clothes make you feel too warm, too cold, or are they just right? You don't have to make a judgment about anything, just passively allow yourself to become aware of how you experience what you're feeling.

Notice the spot where you are sitting. Examine it visually. Explore it with your hands if you like. Is the surface that you are sitting on hard or cushioned? Is it cold? Is it bumpy? Is it comfortable?

What kinds of aromas surround you? Can you smell exhaust fumes, wood smoke, or flowers? Do the smells remind you of another time or place? If so, is the memory a pleasant one? Once again, you don't need to make any judgments about what you're experiencing, just explore how you're feeling with acceptance.

Relax and be in the present for as long as you like. When you're ready to resume other activities, become aware once again of your pulse. Does it seem to have changed from when you first sat down? If so, is it slower or steadier?

Lastly, notice again the quality of your breathing. Do you believe it has changed in any way since you began your experience?

Breathing

Remember that adjusting your breathing may help to adjust your attitude as well. Regulating your respiration helps to supply your cells with more oxygen and helps in the removal of carbon dioxide waste products from the body. And, because of the practice effect, a breathing exercise that you learn in a just few minutes, practiced over time, may have important long-term effects in reducing anxiety, tension, and anger and generally improving your overall health.

Here are a couple of additional breathing exercises you might like to try.

Not only can this first exercise be useful for reducing stress, it is said be helpful in relieving some types of headaches! This technique utilizes an alternating pattern of breathing.

EXERCISE
In and Out Is Easier Than You Think

Sit in a relaxed position.

Place your left index finger and middle finger on your forehead.

Using your thumb, close your left nostril.

Inhale through your right nostril.

Use your ring finger to close your right nostril.

Now exhale through your left nostril.

Then inhale through your left nostril.

Use your thumb to close your left nostril as you release your right nostril.

Exhale through your right nostril.

Inhale through your right nostril.

Repeat this method of focused breathing ten times.

Several bodywork modalities, including yoga, enlist a pattern of breathing known as the "purifying breath" as part of their practice. This way of breathing utilizes the lung's expiratory reserve volume— the air that can be forcibly exhaled over and above regular tidal expiration. Occasionally making use of this technique can invigorate your lungs and be good for your mental and physical conditioning.

EXERCISE
Take a Breather

Assume a comfortable position, either standing up or sitting. Keep your back comfortably straight.

Inhale deeply but naturally.

Hold your inhale for several seconds.

Make your mouth into a little "o" and exhale in a burst of force. Wait for a moment, then see if you can exhale a little more air in another puff. Try one more time.

265

Taking Stock

When people are overwhelmed, hurt, or angry, it's not at all unusual for even insignificant issues and unimportant events to take on a life of their own and appear much more threatening than they actually are. When you're under stress, your priorities can easily become warped and confused.

In these cases, it can be helpful to go back to the basics and examine what really matters to you as an individual. Everyone has a unique and personal value system. Take a minute to look over the concepts in the following exercise. Jot down your thoughts and rediscover what's important to you. You may be doing better than you think!

EXERCISE
It's No Big Deal

I like to think that . . .

O   My family comes first.

_____

_____

O   I'm thought of as a good person.

_____

_____

O   I'm thought of as an honest person.

_____

_____

O   I'm thought of as a competent and successful person.

_____

_____

○ People value my friendship and like to be around me.

_____

_____

○ There's more to life than money and fame.

_____

_____

○ Religion is important in my life.

_____

_____

○ I can forgive myself for honest mistakes.

_____

_____

○ Outward appearances aren't everything—it's what's inside that matters.

_____

_____

○ I give others the benefit of the doubt.

_____

_____

○ I can accept myself, but I'm working to be a better person every day.

_____

_____

Further Reading

Benson, Herbert, et al. *The Wellness Book*. Secaucus, NJ: Birch Lane Press, 1992.

Borysensko, Joan. *Minding the Body, Mending the Mind*. Reading, MA: Addison-Wesley, 1987.

Fisher, Stanley. *Discovering the Power of Self-Hypnosis: New Approach for Enabling Change and Promoting Health*. New York, NY: Harper-Collins, 1991.

Gawain, Shakti. *Creative Visualization*. Berkeley, CA: Whatever Publications, 1978.

Harp, David. *Three-Minute Meditator*. New York, NY: MJF Books, 1999.

Hass, Elson M. *Staying Healthy with Nutrition*. Berkeley, CA: Celestial Arts, 1992.

Hoffman, David. *Holistic Herbal*. Rockport, MA: Element Books, 1996.

Jacobsen, Edmund. *Progressive Relaxation*. Chicago, IL: University of Chicago Press, Midway Reprint, 1974

Knaster, Mirka. *Discovering the Body's Wisdom*. New York, NY: Bantam, 1996.

Lavabre, Marcel. *Aromatherapy Workbook*. Rochester, VT: Healing Arts Press, 1990.

Loehr, J., and J. Migdow. *Take a Deep Breath*. New York, NY: Villard Books, 1986.

Lowen, Alexander. *Bioenergetics*. New York, NY: Penguin/Arkana, 1994.

Mowrey, Daniel B. *Herbal Tonic Therapies*. New Canaan, CT: Keats Publishing, 1993.

Speads, Carol. *Breathing: The ABC's*. New York, NY: Harper and Row, 1978.

Sraswati, Swami Janakananda. *Yoga, Tantra and Meditation*. New York, NY: Ballantine, 1976.

Tierra, Michael. *The Way of Chinese Herbs*. New York, NY: Pocket Books, 1998.

Wells, Valerie. *The Joy of Visualization: 75 Creative Ways to Enhance Your Life*. San Francisco, CA: Chronicle Books, 1990.

Audiotapes

McKay, M., and P. Fanning. *Self-Hypnosis*. Oakland, CA: New Harbinger Publications, 1987.

Masi, Nick. *Breath of Life*. Plantation, FL: Resource Warehouse, 1993.

Miller, E. *Letting Go of Stress*. Stanford, CA: Source, 1980.

Progressive Relaxation and Breathing. Oakland, CA: New Harbinger Publications, 1987.

Ten Minutes to Relax. Manhasset, NY: Vital Body Marketing Company, 1990.

INDEX

A

accommodation, 105
adaptation, 105
affirmations, 156–57
aggressive behavior style, 230–31
alcohol abuse, 75
anger: chronic, 7; control over, 9–10;
defined, 4; history of, 4–6;
identifying and controlling, 43–45;
instinctual nature of, 2–4, 6–7; as
learned response, 9–14; personality
types and, 138–40; reasons for, 22–23;
stress resistance and, 131–32
anger-causing situations, 36–37
anger management tools, 57–59, 138–40
anger styles, 25–27
arguments. *See* conflict
aromatherapy, 174–75
assertive personality style, 234–36
assertiveness: defined, 224–25;
interpersonal behavior styles and,
226–36; lack of, 76; research on,
225–26; techniques, 236–43

B

balance, finding, 144–46
behavior: changing your, 36–40;
cyclic patterns of, 76–80;
interpersonal styles of, 226–36;
learned, from family, 9–14;
threatening, 86–88, 92;
understanding other people's, 56–57
belief systems, 9–15
biofeedback, 172
body language, 186–91
bodywork, 172–75
brain, right vs. left, 129–31
breathing exercises, 162–63, 264–65
burnout, 112–26; combating, 119–25;
red flags for, 117–19;
technology and, 113–14; types of
people affected by, 114–117, 125–26

C

catastrophizing, 51–52
charisma, 116
childhood: *See also* families;
examining your, 17–19; rules learned
from, 9–16; self-esteem and, 153
children: physical abuse of, 67;
stressors on, 107; using, for control, 91
coercion, 90, 92
cognitive therapy, 71–72
communication: blocks to, 218–22;
during conflicts, 250–57;
feedback and, 201–4;
listening as, 179–80, 195–201;
nonverbal, 185–91; problems, 178,
180–85; proxemics and, 191–95;
self-disclosure and, 206–10;
sending messages in, 210–18;
understanding and, 204–6;
verbal, 178
compassion, 153–54
competition, need for, 219
conflict: about, 246–50; handling, 247–57
confrontations. *See* conflict
control: areas of, 90–92; need for, 221–22;
Stockholm syndrome and, 83–89
creativity, 149–50
cultural factors, 30–31

D

debility, inducing, 85
degradation, 84
demands, enforcement of trivial, 84–85
denial, 91–92
directed imagery, 166–68
disinhibition theory, 75
domestic violence. *See* family violence
drug abuse, 75
dysfunctional families: rehearsing and,
221; roles in, 80–83; rules in, 11–12,
68–69; Stockholm syndrome and,
83–89